Green La[n]
and
Kettle Cranes

by
Dominic Reeve

Illustrations by
Beshlie

Foreword by
Michael Holroyd

Lamorna Publications

i

The Author in the 1950's

Lamorna Publications
Yew Tree Studio, Marshwood, Dorset DT6 5QF
www.lamornapublications.co.uk

First published in 2010

© Dominic Reeve 2010

Foreword © Michael Holroyd 2010

Illustrations © Beshlie 2010

ISBN: 978-0-9559832-1-4

Set in 11pt Times New Roman

Contents

List of Photographs and Illustrations

Acknowledgements

The frontispiece photograph of the author was previously used on the back cover of the 2003 edition of *Smoke in the Lanes*, the original photographer being unknown to the author, but thanks are due to whoever it may have been.

The pen and ink drawing on page 175 was provided by Beshlie to accompany an article in the now defunct publication *The Sphere*.

Editorial Note

Romani words are printed in italics and are followed by a translation in brackets. Where a *Romani* word has been used frequently, or where the meaning is obvious, the translation may be omitted.

Foreword
by
Michael Holroyd

To have at least one eccentric parent is often regarded as a bonus for a writer. Dominic Reeve's mother was eccentric in an unusual way: she was, in her son's view, excessively conventional. From his early years at home, and then at school, Dominic learnt how to arrange his life into an unconventional and pleasing pattern. It was a matter of finding out what to avoid. He rejected the philosophy of self-improvement and any dedicated search for financial security. His peculiar style of self-advancement lay in the opposite direction from the tenets of his mother whose hostility he came to see as a paradoxical blessing. Who else could have unknowingly warned him quite so successfully against a life built on the quick sands of lower-middle-class pretensions of grandeur and the imprisonment of respectability (what he calls "the cult of the clothes brush")?

His luck persisted at school where he avoided much unimaginative teaching and compulsory games. He picked up the skills of truancy and an ability to feign illness (which would later come in useful when passing for a manic-depressive as a way of getting out of National Service – a lucky escape for the army). From these difficult years he emerged as a maverick individual, a rebel with many causes, self-taught, opinionated, sensitive to landscape and to writing: a survivor and an escapologist (he was greatly impressed by a chance meeting with Houdini's understudy). It was as if he had struggled out of a too tightly-tailored suit to live a freer, more natural life.

At the age of fifteen he left school and was confronted by the necessity of avoiding the adult world of employment. He survived with the help of some pocket money from his parents and some enjoyable shoplifting. Enjoyment became a necessity for him – but it was not easy for a solitary and apparently unloved teenager to find. His writing grows most vivid and appealing when he remembers happy times, such as wandering through the Bournemouth Pleasure Gardens observing an astonishing assortment of his fellow human beings: the Shouting Man and the pedantic sedentary scholar, the giant gentlewoman with her breadcrumbs and the gays with their adventurous hair-styles and flamboyant clothes. They represent the rich variety of life and many unconventional possibilities. What was necessary, he concludes, was to embrace optimism. All of us are victims of "Chance and Luck" and we have the best chance of making other people happy by being happy ourselves. It is a form of altruistic selfishness.

Some of the most memorable pages in this book are devoted to the Romanies and other Travellers. Finding himself in their company for the first time, he becomes aware that "the feeling of utter happiness was assailing me." He describes them – their animals, their food, their clothes, their faces, their speech, their waggons and also their caravans, their songs, their parties and adventures – with the language of a lover and the accuracy of a scholar. After spending years in a variety of 'Travellery' occupations he settled on becoming an itinerant compost-hawker, calling his wares, ironically, "Best on Earth"! And though he describes himself as "one of nature's oddments" he's a natural writer.

Michael Holroyd, London, 2010

Chapter 1

The Scholar

My first childhood memories are of our family, consisting of my parents and a baby sister, inhabiting a small flat in a suburb of Boscombe, which was itself a suburb of the grander and more opulent seaside town of Bournemouth. The latter, it seemed, always had pretensions of gentility, if not grandeur. To enjoy retirement in such surroundings and to escape the industrialised confines of the Midlands was the aim of many of its denizens.

My father, although a gifted draughtsman, had settled for employment in an office at the behest of his stepfather, in order to achieve the much-revered Security.

Later in life I was to learn that he was the illegitimate son of an old style 'adventurer' who had dallied with his mother and then, upon discovering her pregnancy, had departed hastily for Australia – never to be seen again. Thereupon my grandmother married the man who was to become my step-grandfather and who died when I was about seven years old. Apparently he was quite a wealthy 'self-made' man and, would have made my father, his stepson, his heir. Alas, however, this proved not to be the case: he left my father and mother nothing at all but bestowed his wealth on an unknown nephew instead. I have somewhat unclear recollections of the shock that this had upon my parents but I was still too young to appreciate the full implications. However, in 1937 we moved from our flat to a new house on an estate of *bijou* residences which was being built on the other side of the town of Bournemouth itself.

When we undertook this extraordinary leap into the unknown it was like a new world to me. Utterly different to the close confines of the meaner streets of Boscombe, our new home was situated on the edge of open countryside in a layout of *cul de sacs* and spindly-treed avenues with most of the houses still under construction, seemingly propped-up by the rope-bound wooden scaffolding poles of those times. Many indeed were vacant plots, the houses yet to be erected. Our own, a sort of mini mock Tudor, dark-beamed and grey-washed, stood alone and proud – number 23 William Road, off Littledown Avenue.

It was to be my home until I finally left at the age of 18, partly of my own volition, and equally, propelled by the unremitting hostility of my mother, her fury at my unwillingness to follow her instructions as to the path my life should follow knowing no bounds.

By that stage my father had withdrawn completely from the war between my mother and myself, somehow appearing to regard it as a two-handed private game of charades in which he had no involvement. (It was, unhappily, a strategy that I have myself used on occasion in later life in unyielding situations.)

Upon moving in to the splendour of number 23, pristine and previously unused, I was struck by its wondrous *smells*. Everything was *new* and the multifarious odours of paint, oak staining, and untreated wood, all combined together in a glorious 'muzz' of perfume, the scent having remained with me all of my life.

There appeared, to my young eyes anyway, to be a kind of building frenzy taking place. Each day a 'Sold' notice would appear on vacant plots and, seemingly within days, new dwellings would burst upwards like mushrooms through tarmac. Although no bungalows were allowed in these select surroundings, there appeared to be no *extreme* control over the actual design of the houses. All were different though essentially the same – rather like family cars of the 2000's.

At the age of seven I was a little young for the Big School, which admitted nobody under the age of 10, so I was enrolled at a small mixed school newly opened on the edge of the estate, overlooking the Golf Links. It was owned and run by a pair of mature ladies of indeterminate sex, one tall and thin and the other short and fat, and I spent two of my happiest years there. The little scholars, girls and boys, were almost exclusively from houses on the estate.

Their parents were invariably upper working-class, or even lower middle-class, and within that curious structure everyone tried to enact their own private fantasies. There were, in fact, even a small number of 'common' children attending, though they were not encouraged. The rigid class-structure was all-powerful.

My own mother, although of humble country stock, was a social mountaineer of extraordinary perseverance, if not perception. Should we by chance encounter any of our neighbours in the street, she instantly became a total stranger to our ears: rural shrewdness, combined with cut-glass enunciation of a very dubious quality, brought neither my small sister nor myself much comfort. It was very disconcerting.

On thinking back, however, I can see that it was all part of her plan of self-advancement in a climate riddled with social pitfalls and traps for the unwary.

From one angle her achievement could be viewed with admiration, it being responsible for the presence of a certain theatricality in even the most casual of social encounters. My mother was very dark, both in skin and hair and possessed remarkably glittering black eyes. Her two sisters, my aunts Ruby and Ethel, even darker in complexion, had not, however, attempted to follow my mother in a quest for 'self-improvement.' Instead, they both remained firmly and unashamedly true to their upbringing and roots. During my early years I found their deep Leicestershire accents almost incomprehensible, it taking me some time to attune my ear to their tones. It was rumoured that my mother's father, who died when I was but three years old, was of Romani descent. In his middle years he became a respected horse-dealer, which was interesting in view of his supposed ancestry: he was a Wilson, and there are many families of that name in the north and midlands still travelling about to this day. Both my aunts retained a rather lowly condition of life. One stayed single, and the other married a worker in a stocking factory in Derby, producing one daughter called Joanne, whom I have not encountered since childhood. Their stolid refusal to alter themselves in any way to suit my mother's social leanings did little to encourage any form of closeness; neither side appeared to appreciate the futility of their adopted positions.

On the rare occasions that either of my aunts made fleeting visits to see us – almost invariably during the summer months, in order that they could avail themselves of the desired pleasure of the 'seaside' – their appearance, combined with their almost archaic Leicestershire accents, were to me both alarming and distasteful. The elder, Ethel, alone, swarthy and almost remote, would generally stay for up to a week. She took her meals in her room, rarely mixing with us, so that her presence did not impinge much upon us. This, however, could not be said of my Aunt Ruby, who was always accompanied by my Uncle Eric and their daughter Joanne, a placid, tubby, and entirely uncommunicative child of approximately my own age. Uncle Eric was, apparently much esteemed by the owners of the stocking factory, who employed him as its head maintenance engineer. I remember him as gaunt featured and slow of speech, a small hand-rolled cigarette forever clamped in his thin-lipped mouth. The back and sides of his narrow head were shaved to the skin, whilst atop of his skull, and plastered to it, there lay a few strands of oily hair, gingery and unnatural-looking. Had he been enjoying military service at that time then it must surely have been the dream of any drill-sergeant; a hair-cut to die for!

I could not discuss them with my sister, since, from about the age of six in my case, and three in hers, we were not on speaking terms - a strange condition which remained undisturbed for the next seventy years!

In later times I was to discover the work of D. H. Lawrence and suddenly found dialogue leaping from the page that propelled me back through the years into the company of my aunts' dialect.

It is difficult, perhaps, for those of later generations to be able to conceive of the perils that beset those unlucky enough to experience the social quick sands of the lower middle-classes, and their attempts to storm the walls of the esoteric system and become 'Respectable,' even 'Educated,' people.

Just as today some misguided well-intentioned persons ally themselves with strangely dogmatic religious groups, ignoring the constraints that many such faiths place upon their personal freedoms, so in the past people strove for a kind of bogus respectability. Alas, the following was great in numbers, to remain virtually intact until the wonderful social changes that came so overwhelmingly into prominence during the 1960s.

My entry into the Big School (rather dispiritingly called Bournemouth Secondary School) in 1939, during the month that War was declared, was a fearsome experience. The school, a sprawling red-brick building, was set on a hilltop just outside the town and was, like our little house in William Road, brand new. I was, in fact, among the very first contingent to be welcomed there – it was new to the pupils and staff alike. Unlike ourselves, in those days the inmates of 'Council' or 'Elementary' schools were not expected to wear, nor were they provided with, any form of uniform; thus the pupils presented a rather rag-bag aspect to the casual observer, some from 'rough' homes would mirror the dishevelled looks of their parents and present themselves as miniature scarecrows, yet others of their fellows would be dapper in their 'second' Sunday suits.

It was an interesting sight to see them ejected *en masse* as lessons ended for the day – cloth caps, hob-nailed boots, rough-cut hair, noses streaming. Whilst some, a great social stigma at any level, had necks or faces stained by the application of the garish gentian of violets – the latter being the standard treatment for a ghastly erupting skin disease known as impetigo, a rife and very infectious condition which seemed so hard to treat before the discovery of the antibiotics of today. Perhaps as an unconscious rebellion against the attitudes of my mother, I invariably endeavoured to persuade her to purchase me the kind of footwear and clothing that was favoured by those from the humblest backgrounds – black hob-nailed lace-up boots, child-sized leather helmets, and corduroy 'monkey' jackets being highest on my list. Despite much imploring on my part I never became the proud owner of any such items: all three were instantly decried as 'common,' and thus beneath us.

Strangely enough, although religion played little or no part in our family life, and we certainly attended no church, other less serious aspects of life were invested with more importance than they deserved. The cult of the clothes-brush flourished, whilst the fortnightly visit to the barber by my father and me, to be savagely shorn, became an event verging on religiosity. Individuals who cultivated any tendency to avoid such a ritual, unless they happened to be of an artistic persuasion, were likely to find themselves viewed with extreme disfavour in general, and it was even voiced out loud by those of a rapacious disposition. Conforming was both lore and law.

Once fully integrated into the workings of the Big School I gradually began to feel less and less impressed. Within two years I found myself unable to digest the gobbets of learning that were hurled in our direction by a chorus of ever-ageing teachers. For, as the War progressed, with increasing vitality on the part of the Germans, almost all of the younger staff disappeared into the armed forces. They were replaced by even more elderly, mostly disillusioned-looking men, who had already spent the best years of their lives as school masters and were now being yanked from retirement, with the promise, no doubt, that their noble action could only ensure them further roses in their heavenly crowns!

However, by taking full advantage of a newly-discovered gift for intentionally-comic impressionism, I found several of them more than ripe for impersonation, sometimes, alas, within their hearing.

There was no great merit in my performances but, for a brief period of time, indeed until I was about fourteen, the ability earned me a certain undeserved popularity, and surely saved me from the terrors of being bullied by my more ferocious comrades.

Looking back, over a distance of some seventy-years, one cannot help but feel inclined to the suggestion that some of those ageing pedagogues might well have been prone to bouts of scarce-repressed paedophilia. This was particularly manifested in the person of the Physical Training (as it was then called) instructor. The latter, a somewhat undersized person of middle years with a close-cropped head of grey hair, and cold blue eyes, was indeed suspect. His name was Mr Lice, which must have added to his problems in life, and his manner was very intense at all times. Possibly to his surprise, he was allotted the extra task of schooling our unresponsive brains in the intricacies of geometry and, even worse, trigonometry. Both the latter were utterly incomprehensible to the duller members of the class, myself included.

However, even Mr Lice did not find the subject very endearing and thus would frequently, at a venture, announce that we would repair to the gymnasium for the (to me indeed) dreaded Physical Training instead.

Naturally, owing to these impromptu excursions from the official time table, we had come to school without our 'P.T. trunks.' Hence, to our discomfort, though not to that of Mr Lice, our scrawny little naked bodies were displayed to all. On more than one occasion, and with an even more intense expression in his eyes, he would suddenly, without any warning, discard his own clothes completely, for what he hoped would be our admiration and respect. He would adopt a manly pose and, for some minutes, would endeavour to infuse us with his own obvious enthusiasm for the male body! Speaking for myself, who had never, up that point, inspected the fully unclad form of *anyone,* either male or female, I could only venture to hope that, if and when I was confronted by a female in such circumstances that my reaction would be more enthusiastic – which in truth, some time later, proved to be the case.

These strange activities persisted for the next year or so, on a more or less regular basis. This resulted in no great advancement in my skills in geometry, which I found less and less beguiling....whilst the body of Mr Lice achieved an equal status in my eyes. A short time later he had added an *extra* antic to his gymnasium exploits: at the end of each period he would shepherd us into the shower room, wherein he seemed to achieve great personal gratification from suddenly switching the jets from hot water to ice-cold, at which our already minute members shrank even further, to our acute embarrassment. It was not an experience to which I imagined myself aspiring ever again in life. (Although, having said that, I should perhaps admit to a more pleasurable interlude a few years on, when cooling jets came down on the responsive body, so white and slim, of a young gentlewoman and myself who had taken advantage of the absence of her parents to sport, Amaryllis-like, within the tiled luxury of their enormous bathroom. But that is another story!)

As a hopefully legitimate conclusion to his shower manipulations, Mr Lice (or 'Bugs' as an astute sixth-former had nicknamed him) would invariably supervise a strongly personal inspection to ensure that our 'drying' had been carried out with efficiency. Thus we were each summoned to be 'checked,' lest we had omitted to perform the task to a standard which met with his approval. It was, even to our un-formed minds, a worrying and dubious procedure. The fluttering of the large inquisitive hands of 'Bugs' about our persons brought little satisfaction to us – though judging by the glint in the steely grey eyes of 'Bugs' we may have been missing something. In retrospect it was a singularly depressing experience.

Back in the classroom afterwards, should the air-raid warning sound, we were treated to the sight of Mr Lice donning his red-painted steel helmet, inscribed, "Mr Lice. Head Air Raid Warden." The headgear did him no favours, and resembled nothing more than an upturned Sand Bucket dumped about his ears. It did, however, doubtless give him a feeling of authority should he be faced with enemy action.

He was quite often interrupted by the voluptuous secretary Miss Page during our lessons – thankfully not when he had just performed one of his regular strips. The latter young woman would unfailing bring our concentration to boiling-point as we gazed in a kind of pre-lustful fascination at her mammiferous form.

We were also amazed at the transformation that occurred in Mr Lice whilst in her presence. His agile, once athletic, body would be shaken by curious tremors, whilst his large hands seemed to achieve a life of their own, sweeping in arcs about his person and that of Miss Page. He would seem to perform his own ballet, placing himself in dangerous proximity to the unnerving protuberances before him. One felt that his self-control was in as much danger as when he was faced with us in the shower room. We were, however, too young to appreciate the full reactions of Miss Page. It was left to one of my more down-to-earth fellows, from a 'deprived' background to observe: "If she's had old Wynne-Polly she ain't gonna be worried about Bugs!"

Eventually, on hearing of these un-clad excesses in the gymnasium, the headmaster took firm action, and a melancholy Mr Lice feigned a look of hurt surprise on his haggard countenance, now that his 'enjoyment' had been barred. From that moment he seemed to go into decline and his 'P.T.' became a travesty of its former self, which was a considerable improvement to myself, and all others of a faintly sluggardly disposition.

The headmaster, who had so curtailed the flights of fancy enjoyed by his unattractive member of staff, was himself possessed of a doctorate in philosophy, though of stern Chapel-attending Welsh stock – which always seemed to me, for no valid reason, something of a contradiction in terms.

Dr. Wynne-Parrot was small and stooping in body, with a larger than usual forehead well equipped to house his accumulation of brains, or so my mother told me, awed as ever by any form of title.

He remains stored in my memory mainly for two reasons. The first was his habit of delivering a weekly lecture at Assembly, on a variety of subjects concerning school discipline. If, however, the female teachers, of whom there were four, were banished from the platform before his diatribe, we were fairly sure that it would, even if in a roundabout way, be sexually-orientated. Should the latter be the case the headmaster's Welsh Chapel background would leap to the fore, his arms waving and clenched fist hammering on the nearest table. His staff would sit, stern-faced behind him, their grim features betraying no emotion. The culmination of his tirade would, almost without exception, be summed-up in his concluding "…and *never* before, *never* have I heard of a headmaster having to expound on the subject of…..*filth!* Indeed, *filth!* I can only say that *anyone* found guilty of such things will be *instantly……..expelled!*"

We were never able to comprehend the full measure of his frenzied utterances. Was it swearing? Was it urinating into the little ⅓ pint milk bottles that were supplied daily for our nourishment, deemed necessary for our survival on the scant rations offered to the population, rations of a meagreness not to be imagined by the rotund citizens of today? Or was it, as the older scholars wisely suspected, concerning darker matters, murky and still on the horizon for most of us – though drawing nearer all the time, in fact, to break out like a form of mass hysteria within our ranks all of a sudden with seemingly no warning? Unlike today, our minds did not dwell upon it until it was suddenly thrust before us. It was all very alarming to me.

The second reason for Dr. Wynne-Parrot's interest for us lay in the rumours about his secretary. This little person, whom one imagined to be in her late 'teens or early twenties, presented us with a picture of glamour rarely seen outside the cinema or its idolising magazines. Her hair was long, black and lustrous in its waves; her eyes a deep violet, whilst her mouth was truly a cupid's bow in shape and accentuated by a deep red lipstick. But what most espoused our universal, if immature, admiration, was her voluptuous and generous bosom. The latter, encased with care in a form of bondage rarely glimpsed in suburbia, allowed her actual nipples to be clearly visible to the innocent beholder. Named Miss Page, I was never close enough to her to learn her Christian name, though, like all the other pupils, and undoubtedly many of the aged staff-members, one could but dream! To us boys the respect for Dr. Wynne-Parrot's reputation increased a hundred fold upon his achieving her employment as his Private Secretary. So much, in fact, that rumours began to circulate regarding his sexual prowess: it was asserted by several older boys, that they had entered the headmaster's office unannounced, only to find the hitherto upright Welshman enjoying the pleasure of the recumbent and attractive Miss Page sprawled across the vastnesses of his roll-top desk!

With all the will in the world, however, it was difficult fully to imagine such an event as even a remote possibility. Eventually though, like the later avowed presence of 'flying saucers,' the witnesses grew in number and we began to accept it as one of the anomalies of life. It certainly added a degree of piquancy to his sermons on the perils and degradations of *filth*.

Miss Page herself, remained in the school's service for another two years before suddenly eloping with a youngish plus-fours-wearing History and Geography teacher who had avoided the War, to almost universal disgust, by becoming a Conscientious Objector. With wavy brown hair, usually hanging lankly over one eye, lantern-jaw and looking miserable, one wondered with some astonishment quite what could have attracted the lusty and mammiferous Miss Page to such a joyless person. But, of course, after Dr. Wynne-Parrot he must have appeared quite god-like in both charm and physique.

It all provided us with much inflammatory gossip and would, we were convinced, lead to the mental decline of Dr. Wynne-Parrot who was forced to engage the assistance of a lady from the nearest Women's Institute to take over at least some of the duties previously performed by the rather more desirable Miss Page.

Later, however, even this lady's reputation was sullied when one of the 'common' pupils announced that he had entered the study without knocking, at the moment when the renowned Dr Wynne-Parrot was guiltily pulling up his trousers and remarking: "Very good, isn't it, Hilda. Now go and wash your hands and make me a cheese sandwich!"

Although no other witnesses came forward to vouch for the authenticity of this account, it, nonetheless, became the stuff of legend. In retrospect one cannot but feel just a little sympathy for this learned academic whose reputation for a whole generation of pupils during his headmastership, rested on such uneasy foundations!

Chapter 2

Bombs

For the first two years of the War, apart from the ever-increasing privations of food rationing, our family was not overly affected by its continuing machinations – though rumours of the prospect of greater horrors ahead were rife.

Alas, however, it was not long before we were shaken, almost to the point of disbelief, when my father's age-group – men in their thirties and older – were summoned into military service. My father, Morris, possibly infected by repressed romanticism, joined the Royal Navy. He was ordered to report for duty at a training establishment at Skegness. It proved to be the former premises of one of Britain's foremost Holiday Camps, which had been commandeered by our gracious government – who should perhaps be applauded for their irony in its choice.

My father endured a few weeks of 'Basic Training' there, and then returned to our suburban residence for a week's leave clad in full 'Jack Tar' regalia, at which sight much wonder was occasioned. Indeed, our neighbour, Mrs Mercer, sarcastically enquired, on perceiving his nautical garb; "Have you been on't briny yet?" I cannot recollect my father's reply, though I remember him waving cheerfully at her son, John, who had come home on leave from the RAF just prior to being posted to "Sig-na-pore."

Within months, however, to my great despair, the father whom I loved was posted abroad. His destination was, of course, kept secret from us – otherwise who knows but we might have sent a postcard to Herr Hitler letting him know my father's whereabouts!

At that point I feel that my father should be applauded for enterprise. With considerable foresight he compiled a list of countries, and their principal cities, and for each of them he used a code of kisses, in the form of crosses, which he intended to append to each letter after his signature. It was a scheme which apparently failed to cause any suspicion in the minds of those employed to censor all foreign correspondence sent home by our troops. Thus with a copy of that simple code my mother was able to comprehend his geographical position in the world, thereby achieving at least a small measure of comfort, if little else.

We were quite disconcerted at one point, on carefully counting up the kisses, to discover that he was apparently in Alexandria, when only a few weeks previously he had been no further away than the north of Scotland. Unfortunately my mother's knowledge of geography was sketchy and my own almost non-existent: it was all very worrying, and my mother's dense black hair began to show signs of grey despite her comparative youth. (She did not, of course, resort to any artificial colorants as, at least to the denizens of suburbia on a lowly scale, such conduct was viewed with the greatest disfavour and was thought to be a sure-fire indication of a declining moral code.)

His overseas posting was to last for three years. My father was to return as a complete stranger to me, for he had left when I was twelve years old and not returned until my fifteenth year. I was, however, very young and unworldly for my years. At fifteen I was the equivalent of a ten or twelve years old boy today, with voice un-broken and a childish naivety much in evidence.

From the age of twelve to fifteen the span of years seems particularly lengthy and hazardous in almost every way. In my own case, the change seemed more gradual than dramatic and far from developing the demeanour, so desired, of a young man-about-town, I was thrown into despair at the image that the mirror cast back at me. There seemed little to admire – a lop-sided countenance, big ears, and slightly oriental-looking half-closed eyes, nondescript nose, and a faintly sensual mouth. My physique was rather ill-developed, despite the unwelcome former attention of Mr Lice. Wiry was perhaps the kindest description that I could bestow on it. The over all picture was, to my eyes anyway, acutely depressing and unpromising: all that sustained me was a sense of humour.

The latter, however, was severely tried and tested after I had appeared, more by chance than intention, in a school play adapted for us from one of the *Charlie Chan* detective series which were very popular in those times. The hero, Charlie, was supposed to be Chinese, though in the cinema he was played by an obviously European actor, with a peculiar, rotund, panache; indeed a sort of inflated 'oriental' Sherlock Holmes. In actuality, being totally unschooled in drama, I was only allotted the small part of his 'Number One Son,' which elicited a bizarre and almost wordless performance, and caused much mirth in the undiscerning audience who were only able to envisage me as the person usually responsible for comedic 'takes' on aged members of the staff. On reflection, it is odd to examine the reasons for occasional brushes with even parochial fame: from the moment that production was staged I became widely referred to as 'Chan,' a nickname that I found impossible to slough off until I left the school.

It was my first brush with 'celebrity' status – a condition that I should have recognised as being completely futile and virtually meaningless. Alas, however, experience is not always the finest tutor. One of the advantages of my father being away was that I was left with only my mother and small sister, neither of whom had more than a passing interest in me.

At that time I was perfecting my techniques for avoiding the horror – to me – of compulsory Games, especially football: I found the boys who enthused over its rites mainly to comprise those furthest from my own limited range of friends and to be of pugnacious dispositions and normally our paths would not cross. In any event I managed to fathom out the fact that each week the 'teams' would be picked on the day preceding the 'Sports Day,' as it was grimly called. Thus if one was able to feign illness on that day one would not be included in the list of players. I, therefore, was inclined to bouts of sickness once every week – eventually breaking all records for regular one-day absences. After every day missed from school one was expected to bring an 'Absence Certificate' (a booklet of which was supplied to every parent) duly signed by the parent or guardian, who was required to fill-in the space provided for Cause of Absence, and sign and date it. It was all too easy, and possibly was responsible for most of the events which beset the rest of my schooling. By which, of course, I can only admit – and with some pride – that I soon began to play truant on a grand scale, having perfected the art of forging my mother's signature with ease. I had read somewhere that the forging of signatures is achieved with most success if the name to be copied is placed upside-down and thus reproduced as a *shape* rather than a name. It is more successful than a tracing, which always, in my experience, looks almost too immaculate to be true.

Once I had perfected the technique, however, the world was my oyster. Careful scrutiny of the weekly timetable of lessons would show me the days to avoid, but also allow me to attend on the days on which subjects that I favoured took place. Thus art, English, geography and history were granted my attendance; whereas all forms of mathematics, physics, chemistry, physical-training, or games, faded rapidly from my world.

I suppose that my absences were less noticeable in those troubled wartime days than might have been the case in peacetime. For almost every day we would have to break-off lessons for an hour or two and retreat *en masse,* when the air-raid warnings sounded, to dank cellars beneath the main building, lit dimly, and without any comfort. Better, I suppose, to be buried alive than, if above ground, to be blown-up, or so it was opined by the authorities. Personally I am convinced that those sojourns beneath the school led to the development of acute claustrophobia and fear of suffocation which has been a constant companion for all of my succeeding existence.

Thus I managed to arrange my life into a pleasing pattern which, by one means and another, was to stretch ahead for the next few years until I was eighteen.

Being resident just outside the town of Bournemouth and able by then to ride the rather splendid "Sunbeam Sport" bicycle which my father had left suspended in the garage, intended to remain unused until his return from 'Kiss-land' after the war. My mother, however, always parsimonious owing to her lowly upbringing, had been persuaded by me that it would be more sensible for me to use that machine as it was *there*, rather than her investing in another. (It was not until her death that I later discovered just how thrifty had been her life-style, though I never unearthed the actual *reason* for a lifetime's scrimping and saving: She did not appear actually to be happy at any time that I can recall, which must be viewed as sad by any but the most cynical readers.)

My truancy years were spent according to the seasons, winter being the least attractive – then I would secrete myself each 'free' day in the Reference Room of the Bournemouth Municipal Library and I enjoyed that very much. Given my complete freedom of choice I was able to immerse myself in multifarious subjects, as the fit took me. Art was, at that time, my greatest interest and fortunately the library's stock of literature on that subject was immense and varied. Thus without ever having experienced the benefit of attending actual art galleries to peruse their contents, I, nonetheless, taught myself to appreciate some greatly differing schools and would leave in the afternoons quite weighed down by all that I had studied.

As part of what I was later to realise as an obsessive personality, I would find myself quaffing drunkenly, for weeks at a time, on a variety of subjects – chosen almost at random – suddenly to abandon them and stagger on to something else. Most provided me with interest, satisfaction and actual 'brain-food' – though a spell of attempting to master the intricacies of reading music and playing the violin, all from printed instruction-manuals, left me completely defeated. The complexities had me utterly baffled, and from then onwards my respect and admiration for musicians, particularly those performing the classics, has remained unswerving.

If, during the winter months I found myself able to afford the luxury, in the afternoons I would repair either to the cinema or the Music Hall, of which there were two within the confines of Bournemouth, both of which held matinees at least twice a week.

During what must have been very bleak performances for them I witnessed the acts of people who were either at the end of their careers, or alternatively, were struggling valiantly on the ladder which could, in that most chancy and luck-influenced of professions, bring them undreamed-of adulation, celebrity, and wealth.

The *Boscombe Hippodrome* was the lesser of the two still-existing Music Halls within my radius of travel. It had originally been a rather rococo building when first constructed in the 1880s or 90s during the heyday of such entertainment; but by then, the early 1940s, its glitter was chipped and faded. Nonetheless, for me at any rate, a certain magic still remained.

On a dismal and dank afternoon in January, I trudged from home, after a quick lunch of almost meatless 'Shepherd's Pie,' under the critical eye of my mother – who presumed I was off to school for the afternoon. I had ascertained that there was a mid-week matinee that week, and topping the bill was a very well-known Jewish comedian, a little past his prime, who enjoyed the evocative name of Max Bacon, irony in itself I surmised, in view of his roots.

Thickset, tubby, with small eyes and an endearing leer, he was prone to commence his act with the rather fanciful phrase, "Good day, Ladies and Mantlepieces….."

The latter utterance was, on the afternoon of my attendance, in a sparsely-scattered audience of elderly and semi-infirm Boscombe residents, greeted with very desultory applause and a few occasional titters of laughter.

Professional that he was, however, Max was undeterred and commenced to fire 'gags' at the comatose gathering. His act was to last for twenty minutes duration, it transpired, and his material was mainly devoted to decrying the condition of his body, and explaining how it had prevented him from being accepted for Active Service by the military.

I had noticed an aged couple seated quite near to me, a gap of four or five empty places separating us. A close inspection of them was faintly disconcerting. The man, who removed an extraordinarily floppy cloth-cap with a frayed peak, exposing a pallid bald head with greasy slicks of hair plastered to the sides of his head, was clad in a stained and dirt-caked old raincoat, tightly buttoned to the neck, thread-bare plus-fours, heavily darned tartan stockings, and completely worn-down suede shoes. The image that he presented was that of an utterly decayed old golfer who had turned to alcohol.

His aged wife's features were almost hidden under a faded linen headscarf of no apparent colour or design, an ancient 'beaver' fur coat, and her thin legs were comfortably spaced within tired ankle-length fake-fur 'bootees.'

This was not, however, an outing of self-denial for the two theatre-goers. Both were enjoying the rhythmic inhalation of small cigarettes of powerful fragrance, which they chain-smoked with evident enthusiasm, pausing only momentarily to sink into bouts of hollow-sounding bronchial coughing which rocked their far from stalwart-looking, indeed frail-looking, bodies. Max Bacon was continuing his routine with gusto, nearing the conclusion before a final exit on a song "...so I went for the medical, already, ...I'm standing there, naked, yes lady ...The doctor took one look at me, a lovely sight, lady, an' he sez: "Maxie" he sez, "We've got a new grade for you."

"Wot's that?" I ask him.

"Maxie," he sez, "It's 2f-2f. Too fat to fight!" – at least I *fink* that's wot he said!"

A faint hint of subdued laughter glanced around the audience, but far greater was a hush of disapproval. For the matinee performance at the Boscombe Hippodrome the bounds of propriety had been crossed. My neighbours were in full accord with the disapproval, emitting numerous "Tck-tcks!" of disgust at such blatant an attack on their own pious standards, and puffing even more vigorously on their little cigarettes.

That reaction to such a harmless innuendo, having regard that the first horrific stages of the Second World War were in full spate, has been a lifelong source of mystery to me.

What, one speculates, would such unsung pillars of the lower rungs of society have made of the scripts presented to the public today? Or indeed of the very alarming innuendoes handed out to an extended radio audience by the likes of even Sir Terry Wogan (himself a figure of such solidity as to be knighted by our Gracious Monarch)?

Funnily enough, although my attendance at the Boscombe Hippodrome continued throughout the war, with occasional visits to the grander and much more modern Pavilion Theatre in Bournemouth itself, I had nevertheless found myself being seduced more and more by the cinema. In retrospect I feel that they were my happiest of afternoons (and it had to be afternoons as all my theatre and cinema visits were during actual school time – perhaps lending them a little more piquancy and thrill than if they had been thoroughly legitimate; deceit, apparently, came easily to me).

I was particularly attracted by a tiny and decrepit picture-house, set amidst small shops and back to back houses; possibly the nearest to slums that Bournemouth had to offer. It was called 'The Roxy' and it was the one cinema that I would attend with my mother's knowledge on a Saturday morning. The entrance fee was seven pence in the old money, and a variety of cartoons, Science Fiction, adventures amongst the Planets, (with Flash Gordon as the prime draw for the urchins who attended these morning shows on a weekly basis). Amongst the other 'regulars' was a middle-aged lame cowboy; the latter sported a remarkably large-crowned white Stetson hat and vast leather 'chaps' attached to each leg. His other handicap was his pronounced limp, though this was capitalized on in a very enterprising fashion, and equipped him with the unforgettable title of 'Hopalong' Cassidy.

Far more charismatic than even 'The Lone Ranger' (and Tonto) it was always 'Hopalong' who drew the most uninhibited and vigorous reaction from the short-statured, untamed, audience at The Roxy.

Almost all of those present each week would have emerged from the back-streets surrounding the little cinema. I, although something of a stranger, always went there alone, and struck up some lasting friendships with boys who seemed to want me as a friend. One, particularly, with the appealing name of Ike Pike, was of Romani stock, first generation 'settled-down,' whose grandparents had roamed in the area for almost all their lives, whilst his mother (although having surrendered to the folly of house-dwelling) still journeyed by bus each day to the Square in the centre of Bournemouth where she would stand, with a number of other Romani women, selling bunches of flowers in the street.

In terms of their relationship with their neighbours, I discovered they were viewed with some disdain. This, nonetheless, they parried by a fierce pride in their heritage which, even then, I found very heartening.

Although under ten years old, Ike showed an enterprise and 'push' rarely equalled by his non-Romani fellows and was already occupying a position both of paper delivery boy and occasional freelance window cleaner.

"I don't never axe me mum for nothing," he proudly asserted to me on more than one occasion.

At the morning shows at The Roxy, it was rare indeed if a wild, no-holds-barred, combat did not erupt, particularly amongst those in the first three rows. For seats in those eye and neck straining areas one only had to pay three pence – but, alas, two hours of discomfort did not seem to bring out the best in them and the slightest ill-natured comment would immediately be answered by unrestrained violence, accompanied by screams and curses of an especially unrestrained nature.

In order to counteract this hooliganism the manager, known as 'Old Vic,' would rush from his office carrying a stirrup-pump, and a fire-bucket filled with evil-smelling disinfectant of an unremitting strength and odour, with which he would spray the offenders until, eyes running, dank haired and breathless, they would grudgingly resume their seats and attempt to refocus their stinging eyes on the vibrating screen. During this period of adjustment they would amuse themselves and each other by swearing loudly at all and sundry.

"Like me dead Granny, some of them little cunts can cuss," my friend Ike was wont to observe.

I, of course, was rather pleased as it all added to my private armoury of verbal defence ammunition which would be stored in my mind for future usage.

The more that I grew to know Ike the more I admired him, and his family too; their closeness, easy familiarity with each other, and their apparently shared aims of progress, combined with a contempt and detachment from authority – all those facets seemed to resonate within me, stirring at forgotten or half-imagined experiences in another life. It was very peculiar for me to have such feelings; up till then my reaction to almost everyone I met was of indifference, but not of empathy. Something was wrong but I had not yet discovered what it was; it would take another nine years for that to be fully revealed.

With a wisdom that seemed innate within me when dealing with my mother, I very sensibly did not divulge either my friendship with Ike, and especially not my visits to his home, nor my association with his family. In such matters lies were my only luggage.

Once, I recollect arriving for a visit a little early one day, before Ike had finished his afternoon window cleaning round, when only his mother and ancient-seeming grandmother were at home. In their usual open and friendly manner, they at once invited me inside for "a nice dish of tea and a talk." Ike's mother, Rosina, was more effervescent than her own mother. The latter, however, with her classically Romani dark sculpted features (as I came to recognise later in life) had an imposing presence and strength of character. I noticed that she commanded great respect and that her opinions, no matter what, were always deferred to without fail. Thus she remained seated by the glowing hot kitchen range surveying me intently.

"How come you's friends with my grandson?" she enquired at last. I was by nature a polite boy, which I think appealed to her.

"Well, Mrs Pike," I replied, "he is a sensible boy, we just get on well, and we like having deals together."

"Here, my child, are you sure you ain't got no Traveller in you?" she asked sharply.

I explained my background, mentioning my grandfather and his occupation.

"Hmmm," she replied non-commitally, and spitting into the fire.

"Now then, Mam, he don't want to tell you all his pedigree," smiled Rosina, handing me a cup of very sweet dark tea.

Old Mrs Pike had by then rolled herself a thin cigarette and soon the little room became filled with the acrid yet strangely sweet odour of what I came to recognise as *Black Beauty* tobacco.

The family was made up of Henry Pike, known as 'Bronco,' his wife, Rosina, sons Ike and Bonny, and an older sister Annie. Old Mrs Pike had joined their household after the death of her husband. The latter, apparently, had been a "proper old fashioned traveller" who had scorned the settled-down life-style adopted by his son, preferring to continue roaming, even if in a rather limited area, with his horses and ornate waggon. His widow continually lamented his passing and the house-bound conditions she had been driven to adopt.

Bronco, meanwhile, had taken casual work on the municipal dump, from which he was able to purloin numerous items of 'rubbish' to resell. Their daughter, Annie, had managed to secure employment at a small munitions factory quite near home, which had been adapted from a garage, and to which scores of 'turban' wearing young women repaired daily, earning remarkably impressive wages for the time.

Ike's brother, Bonny, was then only my age, a year younger than Ike. The latter, however, towered above him in height and took full advantage of his superiority of physique. They were, nonetheless, filled with a protectiveness toward each other which I found endearing and enviable. There were, I later discovered, several other families of similar background dotted around the streets of the neighbourhood, all acquainted with each other and many related.

Living myself an isolated and virtually friendless existence within the confines of our own little private housing estate, the recognition of the fact that people's lives were so different in almost every way from the unbending rigidity that I had always known, came as something of a surprise to me. Its artificiality suddenly struck me forcibly.

My friendship with Ike, his family, and some of his friends was, I think, the beginning of a lifelong compartmentalism in my behaviour. I did, indeed, retain a complete secrecy regarding my friendship with Ike and his family from both my mother and also from the other children who lived in our own road, or ones bordering it. Not that I had very much communication with them as I felt no warmth toward any of them, unlike my feeling for Ike and many of his friends. Thus, I was, without qualm or conscience, able to develop my natural-born skills in 'lifting' articles which I fancied from their well-stocked toy cupboards. Those trinkets I would regularly load into the capacious saddlebag of my father's bicycle and transport them over to Ike's backyard shed. It was my earliest lesson in 'dealing.' Ike, of course, being a Romani, was fortunate in that it came as second nature to him. I, sadly, had received no parental guidance in that most maligned of art-forms, but I possessed one of the main requirements; I enjoyed the *excitement* of buying and selling.

Hence our little deals were mutually profitable. If we could not buy from each other we might well find objects which we would *chop* (exchange), which could be even more satisfying. From such humble beginnings, have many a fortune been made"

Both Ike and myself, although not to be admired by some people's rather inelastic standards, were both equipped with our own moral codes which we strove to uphold, whilst those with whom we conducted our juvenile transactions were already, by necessity, very streetwise in their own rights. Thus it was, I was able, by means of such little enterprises, to fund my theatre and cinema-going habits to a hitherto undreamed of regularity, often enjoying the luxuries of being in the *front* seats in the theatre and the *back* seats in the cinema! It was gracious living in its finest hour for a boy of my tender years.

Alas, however, it could not *all* have been beneficial to me. I recollect emerging from The Roxy cinema one cold and misty afternoon in December. It was only four o'clock yet already dim and almost dark and I had a two mile walk home. The film that had been showing was *Wolf Man*, starring Lon Chaney Junior. He was an actor who could represent all conditions of stark fear, suffering, and horror with unequalled conviction. Hence, as the unwilling victim, forced by circumstances to endure regular transmorgrifications from man to wolf, governed by phases of the moon, he presented a truly terrifying image – especially to a lone *boy*, who should not, by rights, have been allowed to enter the cinema unaccompanied by an adult.

As it happened, the result of my viewing *Wolf Man* was so alarming that I became something of a nervous wreck, enduring the journey down the densely bush lined avenue towards home in a state of semi-demented terror, which lasted for weeks.

In my quest for intellectual self-advancement, however, it was about that time that I began reading several of the film-review magazines which were produced weekly then. From these organs of mass culture, I gradually began to realize that the range of films produced was wider than I had ever imagined, and through such reading my taste gradually improved.

To be a child in the 1940's was an experience that few sensibly minded persons would envy. Fear and unease pervaded the country and the fond hope of those who imagined that a swift victory over the powers of evil was a foregone conclusion was soon to be shattered. From 1940 five more years of actual conflict were to ensue, to be followed by almost ten years of what was playfully described as 'austerity years.' However, for me as a child of tender years of age, living on an estate of newly built residences (detached, of course) on the outskirts of the southern coastal town of Bournemouth, the actual war itself was then but a distant fear. It was not until a year or so later that a large part of some pine-forested land adjoining the local golf course was suddenly invaded by a mass of 'foreign' soldiery, turning out to be Americans, that we felt that we were actually involved. In truth, their presence and their innumerable sinister looking camouflaged tents, caused murmurings of dissent amongst the older residents. Their fears and suspicions were further aggravated when it was observed that a contingent of 'darkies' were present, though decently separated from their light-skinned compatriots. Multi racialism was not, apparently, a situation to be encouraged despite the avowed aims of those purported to be engaged in the conflict against Fascism.

Not that I, at the age of ten, was fully conversant with such matters. Interestingly though, I *had* but recently been made aware of the existence of what I was to learn was anti-Semitism amongst several of our neighbours, many of whom were acquaintances of my mother. It first came to my attention when a youngish family moved into a house in our road. I noticed them particularly because, especially in comparison to the other residents, they appeared to be so handsome, even exotic. The husband was a tall and well set-up man in his late thirties, of almost film-star appearance, whilst his wife was dark and elegant, wearing smart and beautiful clothes and showy jewellery. They had but one child, a small and pretty girl of about my own age, blessed, like her parents, with attractive looks.

Our next door neighbour was quick to point out that they were Jewish, with some suspicion, revealing too that they were the owners of several Kosher Butchers' shops. The fact that he did not appear to be in the Armed Forces was, too, held against them. It was very puzzling to me.

Our next door neighbour who was the source of this news was an ancient-looking, unattractive and bespectacled woman with a fried grey perm. She was called Mrs Mercer (I never knew her Christian name) and lived with her husband Stanley and their son, John.

Her husband was a retired Civil Servant from Harrogate; he was bald of head, long of face, and miserable in both demeanour and character. He had suffered a severe charisma by-pass at some stage. Despite those apparent disadvantages, he had succeeded in prospering during his climb through the ranks of the Civil Service. Not only had he managed to buy their house and a 1937 Rover car, but they had conspired to send their only son, John, to a minor public school. To the outside observer, one could not deny, this might have been regarded as something of a social disaster in view of the almost impregnable Yorkshire accents of the parents, whilst the son, surrounded by scholars from more elevated backgrounds, returned home at school holiday times, glowing with self-satisfaction, hair shining with over-generous applications of brilliantine, and conversing in an accent so electrifying and artificial that even Bertie Wooster might have felt a tinge of envy! He did not speak to me....ever.

A little later, he gallantly volunteered for service in the RAF and although deemed unsuitable for flying duties owing to his defective eyesight, was, by virtue of his public schooling, automatically classed as 'officer material,' as was the case in those times.

To the disgust of his mother, it was not long before he was posted abroad to Singapore. She, however, never quite mastered the word and thereafter referred to it doggedly as "Sig-na-pore."

In any event, the presence of their new neighbours did not sit happily with them and they steadfastly avoided all social contact. Even then it seemed strange to me that whole families should be ostracized for no good reason that I could perceive, but just because they were Jewish. One could only presume that jealousy, or envy, were at the root of such prejudice.

Chapter Three

War and Fear

Between the age of twelve and fifteen whilst still at school (if indeed only on a 'part-time' basis) I experienced both the fears and the near starvation of the food rationing of the era, though I must confess that, owing to the secret lack of scruples of my mother, we were not as badly off as many of our neighbours. In that respect my admiration of her conduct in supporting what was known as the Black Market, knew no bounds. Even greater, though, was my surprise in her seemingly innate ability to seek out those engaged in such hidden enterprises. It was by no means a rare event for her to disappear on her bicycle, heading towards the least salubrious, not too distant, neighbourhoods.

Upon here return we would sort through a muddle of food coupons and vouchers which had been removed from the Ration Books of those in financial poverty, to whom the need for cash apparently superseded their need for nourishment.

My mother had always been a diligent and quite expert cook, thus, with the extra ingredients provided by the coupons she was able to continue to produce a fairly tantalizing and varied menu. She would naturally present herself in these matters as being of a generous and giving nature, assuring us that she was helping out those less fortunate, and that it was almost like charity.

As, in those times, I was engaged in almost daily bouts of shop-lifting, slightly dubious dealing with Ike, and a continuing truancy from school, I was scarcely conscience-free myself. It would just have been beneficial to our relationship if she had been more 'open' about her conduct, and shared her undoubted prowess with me.

Honest dishonesty has to me always been a refreshing trait, to be freely exhibited! Many a lasting friendship, in my case anyway, has been so founded.

My father by then had become an almost forgotten figure to me, his location still only vaguely comprehended by reason of his 'kissing' mail. But our next door neighbour continued a stream of questions as to his possible whereabouts, forever continuing to declare her hopes that my father's posting to "Sig-na-pore" was but a matter of time, and that her son John would welcome him with great warmth. As to the best of my knowledge, they had never exchanged more than a few words when we were neighbours, I could not see, privately, any reason for fulsome greetings on the part of either of them should their paths cross.

It was about that time that a rather public domestic crisis suddenly arose at the house almost opposite to our own. A Mr and Mrs Pepper lived there – a couple that my mother had always, from their first encounter, viewed with both disfavour and contempt, largely because Mr Pepper, a sickly-looking person in his late thirties, enjoyed the occupation of a 'Bookie.' Only a pimp or out and out criminal could have brought forth such an ill-humoured reaction in my mother. They were not, she stressed, *respectable* people, and certainly not socially equipped to reside in such close proximity as they were to us.

Quite out of character with the behaviour of the other residents were the amounts of rowdy quarrels which would ensue; shouts and screams amidst the sound of breaking crockery, and even furniture, would rend the air – at all times of the day or even, at night.

This continued for some weeks until, one rainy morning, a small van drew up, and was loaded with a few packing cases and suitcases, into which the portly figure of Mr Pepper entered and was driven away, his destination unknown.

Alas, however, the situation for the local residents rapidly deteriorated – their worst fears gradually being realised. Mrs Pepper, to my own surprise, appeared to become transported into a completely new persona.

Gone were her prim two-piece dark suits and rather coy little hats seated upon her permed brown hair. She was, in truth, of no spectacular interest, even to the more lecherous of the local denizens.

Within days, however, her feat of transformation was complete. It had always been asserted by both my mother and Mrs Mercer that she had long since overtaken the unprepossessing Mr Pepper in years. As Mrs Mercer pronounced, with customary bluntness, to my mother: "Aye, I should say she could give him ten years easily – she's a very hard face, I say."

Mrs Pepper was not an elegant person, rather stumpy and thick-legged. However, she blossomed. Her mousey brown hair, now newly ringlet-ed, had benefited from the application of a rather virulent, yet appealing, henna-red. Appended from her ears were large diamond earrings, whilst her features themselves were curbed from expression by the application a thickness of make-up rarely seen except on the wrong side of theatrical footlights. Should the weather be inclement she would don a white turban-like form of headgear, whilst her body would be swathed in a three-quarter length leopard-skin coat. A knee-length skirt and high-heeled boots would complete her ensemble.

I found her appearance rather attractive, though, upon so remarking to my mother, I was at once the victim of severe admonishment and was forbidden, under any circumstances, to address or even smile at her. All questions as to the reasons for this hostility were parried with some fury, my mother's eyes turning black and gleaming with apparent hatred.

I pretended to accept her instructions, nodding passively. It was the easy way. It was, of course, even at my tender age (especially after becoming a regular reader of the *News of the World*) difficult not to speculate upon the ever-increasing sightings of Mrs Pepper returning to her home, usually in the early evening, accompanied by a youthful member of one or other of the services, and mostly American or Canadian – though occasionally British – strolling arm-in-arm toward her own little Arcadia. They seemed, to my youthful eyes, to display a pleasing affection in each others' company – scarcely a familiar sight to me.

My mother and various of her associates fumed together at this blatantly outrageous exploitation of human desire, and they plotted endlessly as to how they could obtain her eviction – though, as it was her own property, and the forces of law and order were more properly engaged in the fighting of crimes of greater national importance, the progression of their plans was slow.

So far as our family was concerned, my mother was driven almost to the point of apoplexy by one occurrence. It was a dark winter's evening, and the air-raid alarm had sounded so my mother, I, and my small sister had retired to the Anderson table shelter which was set in the centre of our kitchen. It measured about six feet in width and maybe seven feet in length. In very heavy gauge steel and with all sides protected by heavy steel mesh, it was optimistically presumed that it would withstand the weight of the entire house falling upon it without collapsing. Without one there was no doubt of the result – of being crushed or suffocated. With one the risk was reduced by 50% - suffocation was the only danger!

We were all three lying asleep in this cage when we were awoken by heavy knockings of the front door: it was 1.30 am. My mother and I cautiously opened the front door and, to our utter astonishment, came face to face with the make-up encrusted features of Mrs Pepper, her turban askew, leopard skin coat around her shoulders, whilst clinging to her in obvious fear, was a young Canadian soldier of maybe twenty years of age.

"Oh, hello love – sorry to disturb you – but my friend here's frightened out his wits – he's never seen no bombs before, poor darling. Do you think we could come in till the All-clear's gone, love? Be all right, wouldn't it?" Mrs Pepper stood back, smiled and prepared to enter.

My mother surprised even me by the strength of disgust in her voice: she seemed devoid of fear, impervious to the risk of violence. "No you can *not!*" she shouted, eyes black as shining coat. "How *dare* you expect me to let *strangers* into my house. Go away, please." Somewhat disgruntled, and distinctly shocked by this unexpected rejection, Mrs Pepper wordlessly withdrew, dragging her terrified partner with her.

With the sound of German bombers high above us, and the ominous red glow of fires from a ravaged Southampton, some twenty miles away, it having been a continuous target for some weeks, the world seemed anything but safe. Despite such activities, however, my mother felt no inclination to allow such matters to affect her judgement or strange set or moralities. Sympathy did not exist.

Little sleep followed for the rest of that night, my mother's ill-humour causing her to grumble incessantly about the incident, without let-up, until dawn. It appeared higher in her priorities than any curiosity regarding the extent of the enemy's bombing.

As Bournemouth, unlike Southampton, was not viewed as an essentially military or industrial target by either the German, or very occasionally Italian, air forces, we were usually only the recipient of bombs ejected by 'stray' air craft, or those on their way home that had overshot their intended targets and, therefore, felt it incumbent upon them to 'dump' their explosives at random as the fit took them.

I recall once, on a pleasant summer's afternoon, taking a short-cut home across the golf course after having watched a matinee, in lieu of school, at a small cinema in a little suburb of Bournemouth called Winton. There, at the 'Moderne' Cinema, I had spent a happy hour or two watching an early Sherlock Holmes feature starring the remarkably fascinating actor Basil Rathbone, with Nigel Bruce splendid as Dr Watson. I should add, perhaps, that it was actually against my instincts to spend my afternoons during the summer months shut up indoors. Rather did I prefer the seashore or cliff top, lying in a deck chair in the sun and reading whatever took my fancy. Alas, however, during most of the war years the whole seafront, along the entire south coast, was closed off by the erection of immense barricades of barbed-wire of supposedly impregnable proportions, enough, we were assured, to repel all Teutonic would-be invaders. Indeed, in case the barricades were not sufficient to dispel any such foolhardy attempts, they were assisted by a galaxy of sturdy concrete 'pill-boxes' placed at regular intervals, in which machine guns were housed, to be manned on the instant that an enemy fleet was sighted on the horizon. So it was that I was denied my coastal sojourns for the next year or two until, just after our troops struck into Europe, and appeared at length to be proving superior in their fighting tactics, the cumbersome erections were dismantled and the beaches once more became accessible to the public. In this way the towns along the entire coast struggled in their various forms of resuscitation.

In any event, on the afternoon in question, it was about four o'clock. The air-raid warning had sounded, its usual ghostly, quavering, tones so extraordinarily dispiriting, but I decided to ignore it, preferring to wend my way homewards across the golf course, avoiding the immaculately mown greens, and keeping to the heather slopes and little copses and clusters of gorse bushes which were growing indiscriminately as the fancy took them. It was unlikely that even the most dejected of pilots would subscribe to the idea that to cast a bomb, at a whim, from his aircraft upon such a deserted acreage would be anything but folly. Hence I felt quite safe, and rather than bother with an inspection of the sky, would concentrate upon a search for the rare, now almost extinct, Sand Lizard, which at that time still enjoyed a rather limited population there.

After a fruitless search, however, and by then being about half way across the golf course, I noticed two elderly gentlemen, each holding a golf club, accompanied by a dishevelled and beaten-down looking person of indeterminate age carrying two bags of clubs, one on each shoulder. In the days before golf trolleys were invented, there was always a ready supply of such unselfconscious members of the lower orders who were ready to offer their services on a freelance basis, and were known as 'caddies.'

Glancing over their heads towards the peak of a hillock, some five hundred yards or so distant, I perceived what appeared to be a dense grey cloud, mushrooming and billowing towards us in ever-increasing volume.

Shocked, and indeed terrified, I rushed up to the players and enquired, fearfully and in dread; "Look, look – is that a Secret Weapon of Hitler's?"

As the popular press had been assuring us that the Germans were likely to produce one at almost any moment, I felt my enquiry did not deserve dismissal.

The two old men stared with astonishment at the cloud, their caddy followed suit – though with something of the indifference of an aged and over-worked donkey.

"Well, I don't know, my boy," observed one of them, "but it is certainly very peculiar."

However, as the cloud billowed closer and closer and seemed about to envelope us, we discerned, to our unbounded astonishment, that the 'cloud,' in fact, comprised *millions* of tiny feathers!

Our relief was great, and our curiosity greater and we parted company with that combination of feelings.

It was not until the next day that I read a full report in the local newspaper, complete with photographs, of a large Victorian house, amid a congregation of similar dwellings in the West of Bournemouth, that had received a direct hit from a 'stray' bomb and been utterly destroyed.

It emerged that the imposing residence had been inhabited by a single person, an aged gentlewoman, well into her nineties. However, her desire to cling to life had been in no way dulled, and as a private and inventive method of counterbalancing the possible effects of her home being bombed, she had devised a scheme which, by her own reasoning, had seemed unassailable. Thus, with an admirable singleness of purpose and strength of achievement, she succeeded in filling every available space on every floor of her immense dwelling with feather quilts. These would, she assumed, combine to repel the discommoding tremors which might be experienced in the event of explosives striking.

Alas, however, upon receiving the direct hit from the bomb of the lone aviator, each tiny feather secured in quilts throughout the house, had rebelled and broken free from its containment to swirl abroad at will. It was, with some horror, that the would-be rescuers discovered the lifeless body of the aged householder, her death occasioned not by falling masonry, nor other injuries. Rather was her demise the result of asphyxiation – the direct inhalation of feathers! It was, perhaps, my first experience of the follies of judgement which can afflict the very elderly. It was, as usual, the bizarre quality of the incident which remained lodged in my mind.

An occurrence, a year or so later went a long way to confirming my lifelong conviction that we are all mere victims of Chance and Luck during our brief sojourn aboard this planet. (If we could find the key that would allow us some control of either of those facets, we might indeed enjoy a peace of mind which, so far, none of our Organized Religions has, to my mind, been able to provide.)

This incident concerned my weekly Saturday visit to The Roxy cinema, which I attended without fail. One Saturday in July, however, I was struck down by one of the strange ailments which can sometimes attack without warning. I was feverish and shaky, sickly and greenish of complexion. My mother was convinced that it was the beginning of some ominous 'foreign' complaint – almost certainly brought in to the country by overseas' troops.

Hence, racked by delirium and sapped of spirit, I remained closeted in my tiny bedroom all day. My mother, a great enthusiast for patent medicines of all kinds, fed me an unending diet of bread and milk, laced in turn with an evil garlic mixture, an even worse syrup of pine-needles, a malt-based concoction which closely resembled old gear-box oil, followed by draughts of a greyish liquid – the latter advertised as a universal cure for almost every ailment known to man, but specialising in the relief of colic and, strangely, Brain Fever. I feel, in retrospect, that it was a tribute to my mother's previous healthy meals and little else that I survived two days of such intense treatment.

My astonishment may be imagined, however, when, on the Sunday morning, I was awoken with the news that The Roxy had been struck with a direct hit during the very performance which I should have been attending. Fortunately, the explosive dropped was of an unusually docile nature and succeeded only in piercing the elaborately decorated roof of the stoic little building. It was powerful enough, however, to send rafters and rubble pouring down upon the unfortunate little cinema-goers and, although causing no fatalities, a large number of them had to be removed to hospital where their injuries were repaired as well as possible.

My friend Ike's brother was snatched from the jaws of death, from under a tumbling rafter, by one of his cousins and suffered no more than three broken ribs. It was a tragedy narrowly averted, and one in which both Luck and Chance played their parts!

It did, I believe, help to foster the seeds of optimism, certainly no part of my matriarchal inheritance, which have never failed to provide me with sustenance, when faced with adversities of any variety. Those were, so far as I remember, the nearest that I ever came to actual physical contact with air-raids, although I witnessed several direct hits on shops, factories, and houses in the months to follow – but all from a reasonably safe distance.

There was, however, always the promise of worse to follow. The exacting devilry and scientific skills of the Germans was a constant threat.

The whole of our population had been issued with gas masks, in the strong suspicion that such chemicals would eventually be discharged in our direction. Those vile face-masks were supplied in small square cardboard boxes, with a string attached as a kind of makeshift shoulder-strap. They were provided, on set dates, at specified Village Halls, or other Community buildings. Crowds of well-meaning middle-aged ladies were fitting them to the faces of unwilling recipients, ranging in ages from about two to well-worn octogenarians. When my turn came, I found myself forced into this black, rubbery, evil-smelling appendage with a mica viewing window – which promptly steamed-up! This was glossed over at once when I pointed it out, and my mother, myself, and my little sister trudged homewards, displaying our trophies with the righteous pride which my mother always showed when she was *Doing the Right Thing*.

I think it should be remarked that, even in those darkest hours, the British sense of Private Enterprise emerged with vigour and even some inventiveness. Throughout the country little parcels of industry commenced the manufacture of 'Gas Mask Containers.' Of greatly differing design, and material and colour, they suddenly appeared. Bright 'leather cloth' was perhaps the most popular, and fashionable ladies would have several in differing colours to match their clothes. Whilst the more well-heeled would contrive to have them tailored in real leather with sold brass buckles as an added refinement.

Others would display the additions of sporting or aesthetic motifs, to be attached with admirable skill and style. One is bound to speculate on the numbers of Gas Mask Millionaires this little known branch of industry produced.

Strangely enough, even perhaps due to a wariness of reprisals, no form of chemical warfare was used against us in the following years. Hence the millions of gas masks remained thankfully unused, to moulder away until eventually being disposed of as rubbish. Like Ration Books, petrol coupons, and black-out curtains, no longer needed or used, they became unwanted, in our lives.

Chapter Four

War's End

In the1940's the pupils of the council-run 'Elementary' schools were able to leave at the age of fourteen, free to enter the adult world of employment. Fourteen was, and indeed still is I presume, a somewhat alarming age to experience, in a variety of ways. The onset of manhood could be well advanced in some, with sturdy and well-developed bodies if not minds. Whilst others, well behind in the growing-up comparisons, emerged into the wider world still resembling nothing more than children. Thus, despite often attempting to disguise their immaturity by donning trilby hats or cloth caps, an ever-present Woodbine cigarette hanging from their mouths, these unfortunates were generally unable to deal successfully with such disadvantages that life had thrown at them.

On the other hand, those of better physique and stature were equipped by nature to offer their services in a variety of jobs requiring little greater skills than brute strength. Once they managed to obtain such employment its advantages were manifold and their strengths would speedily improve out of all belief.

My friend Ike was one such in development, and he availed himself of the opportunity to leave school with great enthusiasm, impatient to take advantage of the numerous opportunities which he felt awaited him.

By that time he had greatly matured beyond his years and, with jet-black hair, luminous dark eyes, and finely chiselled features, he was on the brink of becoming what must have been the dream of many young maidens, as the perfect man.

Although not then able to drive a motor car legally he had, nonetheless, managed to obtain a slightly dubious driver's licence from one of his cousins, and had purchased a small truck. The latter was a 1936 family saloon which had been 'cut-down' having the rear half of the body replaced by a small open wooden body. This was common practice in those days, before 'pick-ups' were manufactured commercially. Perhaps the most impressive of such 'cut-down jobs' was that owned by an uncle of Ike's who resided in an old showman's van on his own piece of land a few miles away: it was based on the cab and chassis, with truck body added, of a once-splendid 1927 Rolls Royce!

"Goes like a bird, my son," its proud owner would boast whenever Ike and I encountered him whilst out together. He would invariably follow with, "Keep her topped-up wi' oil an' water – she'll soon tell 'ee when she'm out of petrol!"

My own days of 'part-time' schooling were to continue for the best part of a year and my social compartmentalism continued without mishap or discovery. The school, the library, the theatre, the cinema and a little thieving, all had their place; whilst my social experiences became equally as mixed.

My only real friend was Ike, with some fairly close association with his immediate family and even some of his cousins from the locality – who seemed to view me with a pleasing conviviality, even though hints of my slight eccentricity must have shown. However, there was much that I both liked and respected in them all without exception and that, perhaps, shone through. Although the old saying, "There's no love in dealing," held good at all times, nevertheless I was never the victim of bullying or violence of any kind. In truth they were all experiences beneficial for my future – when life did, without question, throw many unexpected situations and surprises in my innocent direction.

They were friends for whom I was grateful, but they made my position at home with my intractable mother and my silent little sister seem less and less attractive. Besides which, having severed my connection with all the other youths of my age on the estate, I did indeed patrol a solitary path. I managed, after a short while, to adjust myself to the singular state whilst in those environs and eventually found that the freedom it offered me was reward enough.

Before meeting Ike I had not realised that the small acreage of Queen's Park was very much an island, intent on pursuing its own path of social dementia, watching the world around it slowly crumbling as even the pit-props of the Old Society began to revolve, in what seemed to be an anti-clockwise direction.

The summer when I left school I had just become fifteen and the whole world was beginning to be more visible to me for almost the first time in my life.

One day I was astounded to discover that it was 'V.E. Day' – the Victory in Europe Day. The War in Europe was over and a kind of mass-hysteria enveloped the land for a day or so, until reality set in, at least. I remember taking a 'trolley-bus' from its terminus near the end of our estate, quite early in the evening, and setting off for the centre of Bournemouth. I had no change for the 3d journey, only half-a-crown which I proffered apologetically to the bus conductor, some of whom were of a bullying nature and would often complain accusingly if being asked for change. On this occasion, however, the ticket-wielding official beamed at me and, with possibly the only generous gesture of his life, waved my money aside in a gesture of astonishing benevolence.

"No, no, that's all right, sonny," he beamed. "It's V.E. night tonight – we'll let you off."

Grand gestures could still be made, even in the lower ranks of the Bournemouth Corporation!

I alighted from the crowded bus as it reached the town centre. I was astounded at the crowds flocking everywhere, of all ages, and speckled with the uniforms of servicemen on leave: they were milling in all directions. As dusk began to fall I found myself meandering down through the Pleasure Gardens heading to the sea. Narrow paths criss-crossed each other, each with flower beds alongside them, and low fencing made of a simple steel lattice-work. As a mark of celebration, for the admiration of the public and the further elevation of their spirits, small honey-pot shaped jars were affixed to the fence every few feet, in which burned stumpy candles. The little jars were in a variety of colours so that the effect could not fail to impress those of an essentially benign nature. Whilst others less romantic in outlook, could but wonder at the extraordinary amount of labour that had gone into providing such a low-key spectacle.

At fifteen, however, I found myself caught up in the spirit of revelry – though despite the presence of small bands of apparently unattached, and obviously frivolous-natured, girls of about my own age, I was not self-confident enough to strike up any conversation with them, even on such a night of universal fraternisation – unheard of before such an event.

Such a disadvantage did not appear to afflict any members of the American forces. Scores of them were mixed in with the crowds, always accompanied by the most glamorous of female companions – many of whom gave the visual impression that they had just walked off the set of an MGM musical! I had never seen their like anywhere in Queen's Park! Hitherto such beautiful and seductive ladies had been firmly restricted to my cinematic viewings: to find that they did actually *exist* was a cause of much wonderment to me.

Thus, although nothing actually *happened* to me on V.E. night it remained as a curious landmark for me.

I was no longer a schoolboy. Life lay ahead – a muddled dream in which only one facet was crystal-clear to me: I would *never* become a nine-to-five wage slave, toiling for others, sadly minus the qualifications for a worthwhile vocation. Within the confines that had been imposed on me, mostly by my mother, I had never been shown the *existence* of any other options in life. A very bleak outlook seemed to be all that was offered to me.

At that time the shadow of conscription hung heavily over all youths, coming into force on one's eighteenth birthday; the rigours of National Service to last for between eighteen months and two years. By some parents it was viewed as an unwarranted interruption in their children's lives, whilst to other parents it was regarded as the means of 'making a man' of their offspring. The children themselves, needless to say, were given no choice.

My father returned home, with an early demobilisation owing to his age and the fact that the European War had ended. As I had been almost emotionally destroyed by grief when he was posted abroad as my love was so great for him, I was naturally looking forward to his return after nearly three years.

Alas, however, disaster struck. The man who returned, smaller than I had remembered, was like a stranger to me. He seemed in no way improved by his experiences of service life, not very friendly, and almost like a lodger. To further my dismay he appeared overjoyed at the presence of my sister, devoting all his time to her, whilst I, as ever, felt alone.

At the moment of his homecoming I was engaged in a battle of wits with my mother as to how I should spend the next three years until I was due for National Service – an event which was firmly rooted in her mind as being the certain Salvation of her son, whose schemes for life were not to be tolerated. No good would come of them, she constantly assured me.

(Privately, I was faintly amused by the thought that if she actually knew the *truth* concerning my activities she might indeed have many more arrows to her bow!)

My father, egged-on with unbounded enthusiasm by my mother, eyes usually burning with indignation and barely repressed fury, did his best to encourage me into taking up some sort of genteel post, perhaps in a bookshop or art materials establishment, as a stop-gap until I was eighteen. Anything, he assured me, was to be preferred to idleness and, to him, its accompanying degradation.

Just about then I was acting out the fantasy of assuming a kind of premature senility, and would be careful to dress each day in a smart grey suit (which I had persuaded my mother to buy, on the excuse that it would be helpful to me should I attend any sudden job-interviews). Thus, that summer I had formed the habit of frequenting, in the mornings, a section of the Bournemouth Pleasure Gardens in which was situated a large and well-stocked aviary of singing-birds of many exotic varieties. Surrounding the aviaries were a collection of rather elegant benches, which, weather permitting, were filled each morning by upwards of fifty ancient residents from local boarding houses, and small hotels, before returning for their lunches at about 12.30.

They were a variable assortment, united perhaps by their one shared characteristic – respectability and a twinge of gentility. Other than that their backgrounds would appear to be very different.

The image that I cultivated for my morning visits was well calculated to cause a fluttering of approval amongst those gathered there. Faintly aesthetic-looking, infinitely reserved in both dress and manner, I was bound to meet with their approval and conversations would be struck-up with differing results. I remember one couple, who turned out to be a retired Professor of Zoology and his bird-like wife. Always attired in a restrained three-piece suit and bow-tie and Homburg hat, this old, rather bucolic-looking person would endeavour to secure the same bench each morning, heaving his considerable weight down upon it with total disregard for anyone of frailer physique who happened to be already seated there.

He would scrutinise those about him with acute distaste. On one occasion, in an attempt to impress him with my (non-existent) scholarship, I began telling him of a novel that I had just been reading, enthusing at how cleverly the author had managed to convey the strictures and discomfiture of life in a slum area of Manchester during the early 1930's.

I was startled, and rather disillusioned, when this learned man, gazing at me with evident scorn observed:

"Pah! If I want to witness working-class life in its lowest form all I have to do is buy a third-class railway ticket to Blackpool or Southend-on-Sea."

He further dropped in my estimation when, on being shown one of my most prized possessions, a book on 'Reptiles and Amphibians,' both he and his wife merely glanced at it before exclaiming, almost in unison:

"Oh no! It is just a *popular* book – of no scholarly value whatsoever!"

I was deeply offended by that, rarely conversing with them again. I did, however, encounter them on one final instance, when I was all but eighteen and I mentioned how close was my conscription.

"Conscription!" exclaimed the aghast professor. "I am surprised to hear a person like you using such a word. The correct word, of course, is *Conscribe.*"

This was said with such contempt that I felt truly humiliated. It was time, I realised, to sever my connection with such an odious, even if erudite, pair.

I then, by chance, became acquainted with an elderly, not very distinguished-looking gentleman. It eventually transpired, however, that he had enjoyed a rewarding career as Houdini's understudy! This was a source of great astonishment to me – but on future meetings he was able to back up his assertions with albums of photographs and cuttings from magazines which proved his truthfulness. In later years I could not help but be mystified as to why a person with such a dazzling career behind him would want to impress some unknown eccentric youth with his past glories.

Another regular at these morning gatherings was the 'Shouting Man.' This strange, rather rotund little man, in his middle sixties I gauged, would enter the Pleasure Gardens and, once inside the grounds, would commence to bellow, at regular intervals, and at alarming volume, "UP THE I.R.A.! – H'UP THE I.R.A!!!!!" Delivered with such astonishing sound and clarity, it would cause even the most stoic to turn their heads towards him in curiosity.

Once seated, however, seemingly unaware of or indifferent to the disturbance that he had caused amongst the ancient nodding heads, he would relapse into quietude.

However, by what exact means I cannot recall, I discovered that if, in an impish moment, when passing his seated figure, one merely half-whispered, "Up the I.R.A!" it would immediately set him off in full spate, and he would vacate his seat in order to continue his strange vocal mission.

Of a rather different order was a wonderful, incredibly refined, old gentlewoman of some six and a half feet in height, swaying and willowy. She was always clad in a long flowing garment, with an Edwardian form of headgear atop her piled-up white hair. Each day she would arrive, accompanied by a smaller and older version of herself, whom she referred to as "Little Mother." They were Mrs and Miss Kimber, permanent residents in a local hotel of a vintage no longer in existence.

Upon their daily arrival in the gardens they would unwrap parcels of bread crumbs and small nuts from black velvet bags and Miss Kimber would set about her morning rites of offering sustenance to the wild birds and squirrels whose habitat it was. Striking both athletic and balletic poses, her arm-span being almost equal to the wing-span of a Golden Eagle, the graceful gentlewoman would eventually become almost obliterated by the mass of birds or squirrels who fearlessly explored her person.

During the summer months when the refinement of Bournemouth was temporarily assailed by hoards of holiday-making factory workers from the Midlands, and even the North Country, she would become swamped by those curious sightseers, for whom such a figure was something of a surprise – an entertainment not commonly seen at home.

A whole mass of other human oddments congregated in the Pleasure Gardens, especially during the winter months. (Once mid-summer arrived the gardens emptied in favour of the glories of the beach.)

In retrospect I think that those years were both happy and at the same time desperate for me: it seemed that life was to alter in a frightening and unstoppable way in the not too distant future when I reached eighteen. As it was, my only ambition then was to enjoy my life and its freedom as best I could: there seemed an infinite pool of astonishing people to watch – why would I want to waste my time in some sort of soul destroying job?

Very soon after the War had finished a large number of discharged officers seemed to flock about the centre of the town, lounging in a newly set-up 'Espresso Coffee Bar,' or emerging from the Dining Rooms of the best hotels. Always immediately recognisable by their expensively tailored garments: almost uniforms in themselves. These veterans, all so healthy-looking, well-groomed, and forming a distinct class of their own, favoured beautifully tailored hacking jackets, cavalry twill trousers, and *always* suede chukka boots.

In winter there might be added a check flat cap and an 'officer's warm' overcoat. The more dashing of them seemed to perceive the opportunity offered in the extremely profitable field of used cars, mainly of the sporting variety, some even opening their own showrooms. From the distance of years my fascination and envy of them was immense.

It was a long way from the world of Ike, which I had cultivated so happily, or indeed my lapses into premature senility! This was the time when I suddenly became aware of the presence of predatory gays (or 'queers' as they were then called). As a loner I had not discussed the subject with anyone at all so I was not sure whether the occasional importuning which I received was a common happening to others of my age. Even I, however, was aware that in certain areas of the town 'it' was a haunt of such men – generally conspicuous by their obvious pre-occupation with their appearance, of their adventurous hair-styles and flamboyant clothes. Visually I found them a refreshing alternative to the depressingly drab attire, and mown hair, of the male inhabitants of my own area of habitation, where any faint adventurousness displayed in similar manner was considered a gross breach of etiquette, and most certainly not to be encouraged.

In the process of my long and solitary perambulations along the sea shore, the cliff tops, or the Pleasure Gardens, it would be no unusual occurrence for me to be accosted by one or more such individuals, generally in their thirties or forties, all instantly easy to pick out. Strangely enough, despite various facets of both my appearance and personality, I never felt drawn to them in any but the most superficial way. Despite their obvious desire to tempt new and inexperienced youth into their circles, they were not for me. The most extreme examples did, of course, arouse my interest slightly from a pictorial angle – but I otherwise shunned them whenever possible.

I do recollect being utterly fascinated by one spasmodic visitor to Bournemouth, who appeared at intervals during both summer and winter. He always resided, without fail, at the largest and most expensive hotel in the town – a vast, rococo, building overlooking the sea.

It transpired that he was a member of the socially exalted Tennant family, with sufficient private funds to enable him to live his life, in chosen lone splendour, under circumstances of unrivalled luxury.

Like all of the Tennant family whose pictures I have ever seen, this apparently unsociable member was gifted with the kind of dashing looks and stature that could not fail to be admired. Maybe six feet two inches tall, with fine almost Grecian features, crowned by elegantly long blonde hair, he was always immaculately dressed with numerous suits tailored to his wishes, though more theatrical than clerical, with the addition in winter months of heavy, camel or Crombie, overcoats.

In an effort, I presumed, to offer a more carefree-looking image to the world he would almost always, during the cold weather, sport a continental-looking black beret and a striking mauve scarf of a generous length, thrown about his shoulders.

To accentuate, in the eyes of most of the more respectable of Bournemouth residents, the dubiousness of his character, he was gifted with a peculiarly smooth small-gaited walk – as though on wheels. Such indeed was his own kind of charisma that fellow pedestrians would fall aside in wonder whenever they encountered him.

I never had either need, nor indeed opportunity, to converse in any way with this agreeable looking figure – and, owing to my own later movements, he gradually faded from my memory.

Much later in life, however, when enjoying an unexpected encounter with a young woman of extraordinarily elevated social position, the Tennant family name came up. It was thus, with some sorrow but no *great* amazement I learned that, having taken to residing in the South of France, he had eventually become so bored with his hedonistic existence that he had taken to his bed in disgust and remained there, easing himself gradually from this planet.

It was then that my own greatest desire in life was to be in receipt of what was referred to as Private Means. To me it seemed the answer to all my problems. Not that I was greedy or over-ambitious in my aims; just enough to lead a frugal but *free* life was all I wished for.

I was, in fact, though only semi-conscious of the fact, leading a form of that very life then. I was given a very small amount of pocket money by my unwilling parents – with assurances on my part that I would be industriously seeking even a humble form of employment rather than be 'idle.' Actually, it never even crossed my mind that my life truly fitted such a category. I was fully taken up by the observation of interesting people, a little shoplifting, and my continuing secret friendship with Ike and his family.

Ike and his brother, who had then left school too, were concentrating in their formation of a scrap-metal business and a little 'General Dealing.' Despite petrol and other rationings they themselves seemed to be unaffected by such matters. They had but recently managed to rent a small yard and two lock-up garages and so they were able to expand their interests and investigate new avenues of business. I always tried to supply them with untraceable and easily disposable objects and so it was rare indeed that they turned any of my offers down.

It gradually came about that I seemed to be spending more time with Ike's brother Bonny than Ike himself, who had plunged full-time into his business ventures. Bonny was in many ways a reproduction of Ike, certainly physically, though mentally not possessed of the innate dynamism that characterised his brother. We became very good friends, often embarking on minor thieving exercises together, without the disadvantage of ever being apprehended. I continued to visit their home once or twice a week, becoming more and more drawn into the complications of their family matters. Sometimes, and usually a welcome surprise, relatives of theirs would drop-in unexpectedly. It transpired that most of them were Rosina's brothers or sisters, or sometimes cousins. It seemed a rarity that anyone totally unrelated would call. The majority were dark and of a cultivated, yet slightly run-down, appearance. I was always struck at the manner in which they seemed more than anxious to court my acquaintance. On occasions their conversations amongst themselves would throw-up words unknown to me, foreign-sounding.

Old Mrs Pike, usually referred to as Aunty Kizzy, would, on hearing such words, cry out, "*Kekker rokker – dik* the *chavi*." Her gaze would fall on me, and the speakers would stir uneasily. That, of course, was in my early days: I later became conversant with their use of the 'foreign' words, learning them to be *Romani*.

It was not to be too far in the future that, through the ministry of Ike and Bonny, I began to use the speech unselfconsciously in all my conversations with the family, and indeed their relatives too. A form of communication which was to become indispensable to me during my life ahead.

Although it was never actually stated that I was a Romani myself, there was a kind of thinly-developed tacit understanding that I was, even if from two generation before, connected by more than casual chance to the life and aspirations of Travellers. Even old Mrs Pike would eventually, laughing at something that I had said, observe:

"My child, you'm just like a Traveller – like me dead Mother you is!"

"I wish I was," I would smile, and so I would be the recipient of grins of appreciation, especially from the dark and ravaged-featured elders, who seemed, in some way, to understand my motivations which was in itself a source of gratification to me.

Their talk was more than interesting enough for me, strange epithets and descriptions filling the fire-warmed air in the little kitchen--living room – summer or winter the wood fire was always burning, often with heavy iron pot, or gracefully-shaped iron kettle suspended from a chain in the flames. A fascinatingly scented stew would seem to be forever within its grasp.

"What you got in the pot, rabbit-stew, Aunt Kizzy?" visiting relatives would enquire with a smile.

If feeling in a mood of jocularity old Mrs Pike would reply, without hesitation, her black eyes gleaming with mirth, "That's cow's cunts an' cauliflower, my child!"

This would never fail to arouse much amusement from all ages of listener.

It was, however, a comment which, if repeated to my mother was one with which she would find no reason for either laughter or applause! Yet to me it was just a part of a loving and unrestrictive or uncensored family life that fate had denied me.

There was a certain irony in the forms of existence in which both their family and my own had become enmeshed – neither entirely at ease within their circumstances, into which they had allowed themselves to be drawn.

The Pike family, and their relatives, were all Romanies, still restless, unwilling to accept a way of life that was ruled by the petty authority that is accepted by and large in society – no longer enjoying at least the *myth* of the Free Life, and missing their horses and waggons, their outside fires, and their frequent movement.

On the other hand, by many standards, my own parents were not *settled* in their brand new *bijou* villa, with its mock-Tudor pretensions, and the pillars of class segregation, and the essentially Saloon Bar mentality an almost universal condition. Unlike the Pikes, however, most of the residents did not even have the solace of pining for a fondly-remembers past with which to comfort themselves. It seemed a faintly pointless journey.

The significance, and rewards, of a heritage of pride was hammered very strongly into my consciousness by an event to which I was soon to be invited by the Pike family.

It was an invitation to the eightieth birthday party of old Mrs Pike, Aunt Kizzy, and was deemed of great importance – the fact that I was asked was a matter of extreme pleasure, gratitude, and flattery to me – the only *gaujo* (non-Romani) to be present. I was deeply troubled by what form of present I should take, and ventured to ask Ike's opinion.

"Me granny'll be happy as a lark to see you – any little thing'll do," he rather unhelpfully replied.

I had noticed, however, that it was obvious that she possessed a great love of rings: each finger of both hands was decorated by a least one, often two. On her right hand they were all gold, sovereigns, half-sovereigns, 'plaited', and 'horseshoe' rings. Whilst her other hand sported only silver ones, again all large and elaborate.

By chance that day I had noticed a very 'Travellery' silver ring, impressive in size and shaped in the form of a belt, with a large horseshoe buckle.

My mind sprang back to it at once and I hurried to the shop where I had seen it – hoping that it had not been disposed of. The shop lay at the end of a back-road behind the main street in Boscombe. Small, with mesh-protected windows, it traded under the somewhat provoking title of The All-Sorts Shop and was owned and run by Fat Sid. The latter, grossly overweight, balding, and probably in his early thirties, was not a sight to cause female hearts to flutter. Yet despite his apparent handicaps he nonetheless had secured for himself a remarkably attractive live-in partner. Named Yvette, she was small, voluptuous, with cornflower blue eyes and luxuriant blonde hair of some three feet in length. Only, perhaps, the ever-present cigarette dangling from her enhanced lips, and her nail varnish of a dense blackness, gave clues as to the reason why she may have indeed possessed more affinities with Fat Sid than were at first apparent.

They were the first 'fences' of my acquaintance, and we seemed to sustain a kind of restrained friendship, though in those days, of course, my ability to defeat them in the small battles of haggling in which we always engaged, were rarely successful. In retrospect I realised that they always left me *just* enough profit in those matters to make it worth my returning.

Their stock was truly multifarious, changing weekly at a remarkable rate.

A glance in the left hand side of the window, however, showed me that the buckle-ring still nestled there.

I entered the dimly-lit, low-ceilinged, little shop to be confronted by the double firing-power of both Fat Sid and Yvette. The latter was seated cross-legged on a kind of chromium framed bar-stool, as ever smoking languidly. She wore a ruffled white blouse, and a scarlet pencil-slim skirt of a cut more than sympathetic to her lower body shape. Her shoes, block-heeled, peep-toed, and ankle-strapped, matched her skirt colour exactly. I found her a vision of taste and excitement.

"Hello, darling," she smiled, in a rather detached way.

"All right, cock?" Fat Sid greeted me, his tiny pale eyes darting over my person.

"What can we do you for, cock?"

"Well, you know that old ring, the silvery buckle-belt one – how much do you want for it?" I asked.

"Oh! Do you hear that, Yvette, old silvery one!" he grinned coldly.

"Oh! That old silvery one – Oh, he knows what he's on about, eh, Sid?"

"I tell you what, cock, seeing as how it's you – you can have the ring for eight pounds, an' he's hall-marked."

"No, I haven't got that much to spend," I assured him, with the innocence of youth.

"Oh, poor little thing," breathed Yvette through a cloud of blue smoke.

"Well, what have you got, cock?" demanded Fat Sid, giving every sign of becoming ill humoured.

"I've got four pounds – that's all I *have* got," knowing that I had in fact the total sum of five pounds on me.

"Well that's no fuckin' good is it – ain't you got nothing you could put with it to make the money up? Somethin', *anythin'*, an' I'll try to have a bit of trade – even tho' you ain't brought me nothin' lately, have you, cock?"

I suddenly remembered that I had about my person a rather attractive Parker fountain pen that I had 'obtained' the previous day. I brought out the pen, which was a fetching array of mauves and lilacs, with a gold nib, the whole concealed in an attractive little case.

Fat Sid took the pen in his stubby fingers, eyeing it with no sign of approval. He handed it to Yvette who, to my mystification, winked at me, then at Sid, and wordlessly handed it back to him.

"Gimme that pen an' a five-pound note an' you can have the ring," he announced with an air of finality.

Even in those days I felt that the humbler course might be the most likely to achieve my desired result. It was not, I judged, the time for the, "I tell you what I'll do – I'll give you £4," approach. Thus I looked as sad as I could and assumed what I hoped was an expression of regret.

"If I had £5 I would give it to you," I mournfully admitted, "but I've only got £4 with me – which I'll give you now. Any money I've got at home is already spoken for. Sorry, but that's the best I can do."

Fat Sid's rather expressionless features suddenly creased into what for him passed as a smile.

"He's a trier ain't he, Yve?" he grinned at her, receiving a faintly quizzical response.

With that he stumbled breathily over to the window, picked out the ring and handed it to me with a grunt, grasping the pen from the front of the counter and hiding it away.

"Warm, cock?" he grinned at me as a parting shot.

"A bit," I admitted, leaving to the sounds of Yvette laughing and coughing simultaneously.

As I left the premises of Fat Sid, the buckle-ring safely stowed in my waistcoat pocket, I headed for home.

Rounding a corner I suddenly became aware of the presence of a long queue of shabbily-dressed women, mostly in headscarves and drab overcoats. It soon became clear that their mission was to await the imminent opening of a fish shop. Fish was not actually rationed then, unlike almost all other food, and became available at completely disorganised times – whenever a shoal had been landed locally by the few rather elderly fishermen still manning their nets.

Realising its rarity value, and having been well schooled by my mother in the advisability of joining *any* form of queue whenever one was encountered, I stood within its ranks.

Immediately in front of me were two women, one still retaining a faint vestige of what might have once passed for girlish charm, now about twenty-five or so; the other, older, lumpy, round and squat, with putty-like undulating features. They were deep in conversation.

My interest was captured suddenly by the words of the older woman: "……you remember, she had that black Yankee soldier boy friend – black as the ace of spades. Well, I seen Doris yesterday an' she told me as she've had the baby ……… Oh yes, well anyway 'tis a boy. An' do you know what? He've turned out to have one white arm an' one *black* one, *an'* one *white* leg an' one black one! Doris sez she ain't never seen the likes."

Hastening to avert my gaze, knowing the natives of that area to be more vocal, should they feel their aural privacy being invaded, in their aggression, than anyone from Queen's Park would be, I took a step backwards – before focussing my mind on the piscatorial dining pleasures which I hoped lay ahead.

Chapter Five

The Birthday Party

The day of Aunt Kizzy's birthday party was set for the following Sunday and, according to Ike and Bonny, a goodly attendance was promised both from local relatives and friends, and also from those from quite long distances away – some still itinerant, others settled-down either on their own land or in council-provided housing.

This was just before the return of my father from abroad, thus I still had just one adversary to combat when planning my movements. I did not, of course, apprise my mother of my destination that Sunday, inferring that I would spend the day walking to Sandbanks, a bordering area of unequalled luxury and wealth. This appeared to satisfy my mother's rather faint interest.

It did, however, by no means fail to evoke her approval when she noticed that I had donned my best dark grey suit and suede shoes, a blue and white polka-dot tie completing my refined tailoring. Lies, as ever, my only luggage.

The event was fixed to commence at about three o'clock, after the closing of the public houses. It was still in the days when Travellers were not reticent about displaying certain motifs which singled them out at once. The men, almost without exception, sported silk *diklos* (neckerchiefs) knotted at the throat, the older ones often preferring them worn cross-wise with the ends tucked into their waistcoat lapels. Pure silk was always the preferred fabric. At that time, too, the fashion for hats – usually wide-brimmed trilbies in dark colours – was at its peak; quite frequently boys of ten or twelve would don suits like their fathers, and hats too. Self-confidence oozed from those Little Men, to the pride of their parents. It was in no way uncommon to see them puffing away on roll-up cigarettes, or even cigars! Such behaviour was rarely discouraged and was regarded by many as a private form of infection-warfare.

"They fags kills them old germs," they would optimistically assert.

The suits of the men were invariably tailor-made, preferably by tailors familiar with the requirements of such customers.

It was a curious kind of mongrel design, drawn from both Hollywood and the more rarefied influences of the Norfolk jacket, and even the classic Hacking jacket of the 'County' set. Many-pocketed, half-belted, and yoke-backed, as was the essentially sporty style, but, for the Travellers, it was always made in more formal cloths – serge, gabardine, or flannel being much favoured, often in pin-stripe or rather restrained plaids. This was, of course, a time before the advent of the 'drape' suit of the 1950's, or the later splendours of the exciting 'Teddy Boy' extravaganzas. Suddenly, dressing for men became fun, no longer locked within the cautious limits prescribed by the Tailor and Cutter!

I decided to walk to Ike's, rather than undertake the journey by bicycle, with the attendant difficulties of parking it safely within the area of Ike's house.

I judged that it would take me about half an hour, which proved to be correct. Upon nearing the little house, however, I was utterly unprepared for the sight which faced me. On each side of the road, for fifty yards or more on either side of Ike's home, there were parked a motley collection of vehicles, even two horses and flat trolleys, with old overcoats flung over the horses' backs. On all sides of them were motors; old saloons, numerous 'cut-down jobs' of some dilapidation, two large pre-war Bedford 30cwt vans, and four or five old scrap-dealers' lorries. Any one of them, on its own, might have passed for the workhorse of a jobbing builder or suchlike artisan. However, parked together in this way their individuality seemed to fade away as they inevitably assumed the Traveller-look – indefinable yet un-mistakeable to those of a kindred spirit.

As I neared the door I could hear music from inside the rear of the premises – an area which I had hitherto not been in a position to view.

Bronco himself was standing at the front door, clad in a brand new navy-blue suit, Traveller-style, elastic-sided boots, and a black and white paisley neckerchief. His pitch-black hair was oiled and slicked-back with some care, and he smiled a welcome.

"Come in, my boy," he said. "Go on through – Ike an' Bonny's in there an' me Aunt Kizzy too, if she ain't fallen over *motto* (drunk) yet!" We laughed and I passed through the kitchen and then through the door into the main room.

Once inside this hitherto unknown place I was rocked with astonishment at what met my gaze.

The room was almost filled with people, all Romanies, and many obviously related. Ranging in ages from babes-in-arms to really ancient men and women, the latter mostly sipping on glasses of beer or spirits, the atmosphere still retained something of the cautious *bonhomie* and restrained utterance, which invariably disappear in such circumstances after an hour or so. I felt much as I imagine a canoeist must feel just before shooting the rapids: excitement mixed with slight foreboding. But before I could allow myself to be taken down by such thoughts I was hailed by Ike and Bonny.

The Birthday Party

They called me over to where they were sitting, with two dazzlingly attractive girls, each with sparkling eyes and jet-black hair drawn back in braids. They fastened unblinking stares on me, which, alas, did little or nothing to engender a blossoming of the light badinage which I felt must have been expected of me.

Instead, catching sight of the almost hidden figure of Aunt Kizzy, I moved across the room, to where she was sitting in front of a glass display cabinet filled with Crown Derby and Royal Worcester china, surrounded by an assortment of rather elderly men and women, talking animatedly together.

To my relief, as I grew closer, old Mrs Pike caught sight of me and beckoned me to her. She was in impressive form, her dense white hair coiled around her head, a fine pair of heavy gold drop earrings shone, and a gold necklace adorned with at least a dozen gold sovereigns and a similar number of half-sovereigns, nestled at her throat. It was good to see.

Dressed, as always since the death of her husband, in unyielding black and neat little button-boots, she was indeed a wonderful and dignified matriarchal figure.

I had wrapped the buckle-ring in a piece of silver paper and I surreptitiously handed it to her, at which her eyes lit up in an almost childish expectancy.

"Just a little gift for making me so welcome in your family," I said, rather lamely.

By this time, however, her nimble old fingers had unwrapped my offering and she had it displayed on the palm of her hand.

"My dear son, you'm so welcome as the flowers in May," she said enthusiastically. "My two gran'boys thinks a lot of you – an' that's good enough for me. I thanks you for me ring – an' he shan't leave me finger till they puts me in me box!"

I was knocked a bit askew by these sentiments, but instinctively knew that whilst I remained in favour with old Aunt Kizzy that my welcome was assured.

On the excuse of going to get another drink I momentarily wandered across the room. What struck me most forcibly was the feeling of utter happiness that was assailing me, the reason for which I was finding a source of great puzzlement. For though I was a lone oddment amongst a collection of people all known to each other, and mostly related, I was in no way being treated like an outsider. Although some were obviously curious about me I received no badgering, only the most amiable conversation being thrown my way. I returned to Ike and Bonny, the girls having vanished, who were in the company of four or five of their first cousins, two of whom were locally settled-down and two of whom were travelling about – still with horses and waggons.

I was greatly intrigued to learn the names of the cousins to whom I was introduced: Jobi, Toby, Libby and Marky. All four were hovering around their late teens, well-built and smartly dressed in Traveller-style dark suits and coloured neckerchiefs. They smiled slightly shyly at me, and there was a curiously child-like good humour about them: only their eyes, hard-looking in repose, gave them the 'edge' that would stand them in good stead during the lifelong battle for economic survival amongst *gaujes* which lay ahead for them.

Ike, Jobi and Toby were all new to the joys of motorisation, and each waxed enthusiastically about the merits of their respective vehicles. Even then I realised that each one's boast of the prowess of his particular vehicle was but a preamble to an offer to 'chop' (exchange) it for one of the others' motors – money going either way, as an incentive to the deal being struck. It had long been the custom of Travellers to exchange their horses with each other, and it was soon to apply in the same way now that they were becoming mechanised.

The formalities of insurance change-over, necessitated by law, sometimes took a little longer to understand.

The walls of the room, as is often the case amongst recently settled-down Travellers, were almost entirely covered with enlarged black-and-white photographs of past generations. Gnarled and ancient men, faces cratered, pitted, and scarred, peered out from beneath pulled-down black hats, with either a clay pipe or a thin cigarette clamped in their mouths. Or aged women, whose faces seemed even more badly-served than their men folk by the outdoor life, combined with the toasting effect of over-close proximity to the wood-fires on which they cooked in the face of the elements. These relics of a not too distant past, their images preserved in cut-glass or ornate silver frames, were there for respectful inspection by their descendants.

In other less exotic frames were pictures of bygone splendours in which whole families were gathered in front or beside tall and densely carved old Reading Waggons and smaller barrel-topped ones, and other pictures of fine horses, some with Romani youths riding bareback with a natural grace and beauty. There were even pictures of well-loved lurcher dogs, varying in size from cross-bred whippet-Bedlingtons to larger breeds of Deerhound cross greyhounds – mostly rough-coated and yet elegant, all built for stamina and speed.

Seeing my attention on the photograph of a small but especially well-shaped animal Bronco remarked:

"That was me dad's dog – the best dog in Hampshire. Send him out in any field an' he'd surely turn a hare, s'help me, God."

I was overcome by the fascination of every aspect of the birthday party – the family, the visitors, the colour, and the ever-present glint of gold from the women's jewellery to the mouths of most of the men.

Jobi-boy's father arrived just then, a little late, and entered smiling broadly to display two new tomb-stone-like gold front teeth.

"I likes them new gnashers, Jobi," said his cousin, who had not seen them before.

"Ah," rejoined Jobi, "me Uncle Nelson said: 'Put your money where your mouth is' – so I did!"

Much merriment ensued at this rather ingenious quip, and the party began to liven up.

By the time that the early evening had arrived Rosina and her daughter, helped by some of the aunts, began loading food of all kinds on to a long trestle-table which they placed along one side-wall. Despite the food rationing being the ruination of most people's entertainment, there seemed no shortage in this ostensibly mean little house. Roast chicken, pork, sausages, and even pigeon and rabbit were served in profusion. Hand made brown or white bread rolls were available and even modest bowls of salad were offered. Within that period of time it was a truly wondrous spread. No sooner was the table laid than the guests showed their appreciation by falling on it like gannets, flatteringly clearing the table of its entire contents, apart from the salad, within ten minutes.

"My God, them *kanis* (chickens) is *kushti* (good)," enthused a large, fat, blonde woman whose capacious bosom was all but obscured by the assortment of gold necklaces and strings of gold sovereigns that lay comfortably upon it.

As soon as the guests had consumed the food the whole room, which was enlarged by a rear corrugated-iron extension which Bronco had recently constructed, was cleared as much as possible, and a gramophone and loudspeaker were placed on a low table in one corner.

No Traveller's party, I was to learn, was complete without both dancing and live singing.

During the early part of the celebration the singers taking to the microphone were, by and large, rather restrained in their renditions of popular songs – a restraint which was rapidly to disappear as the evening wore on.

It was the first time in my life that I had attended a Travellers' party of any kind, so its affect on me was to bring about a condition of undiluted euphoria and an equal measure of astonishment.

Fresh from years of the constraints of lowly suburbia, and considerable loneliness, I would never have been able to *imagine* such a scene, in which all seemed to blend together in the pleasure of each other's company, all intent on pursuing the elusive 'Good Time' and all that it entailed.

Several couples had taken to the floor and were performing rather sedate dance-steps together – for, of course, it was prior to the years of reckless abandon which were to follow with the appearance of 'Rock and Roll.'

One of Rosina's younger sisters was standing at the microphone, her braided hair and long plaid skirt, not to mention her heavily be-ringed fingers and variety of gold necklaces and brooches, seeming faintly at odds with the ballad she was singing. The latter more usually heard being performed by a broadcasting star of that era, namely a rather buxom young woman called Anne Shelton.

However, the singer was in good voice and was appreciated by her audience. As she concluded her place was taken by a very old man, whose cultivated appearance, white hair, and pencil-thin moustache hinted at a past of romantic adventures.

"Orders! Orders!" shouted a man in a Prince of Wales check suit and a trilby hat.

"Oh my dear God above," said a man near me to Bronco. "Hark! Here's me dear old Uncle Abraham – he could sing 'fore tunes come out!" I was not sure whether this counted as praise or not, but his preparation to sing seemed to be met with mounting enthusiasm by all present.

"He'll sing a proper old Romani song – like me dead farver he will," pronounced Ike's Uncle Alfie, in a thick voice racked by a bronchial cough.

Like a born performer the aged Abraham smiled at his audience, and slowly commenced to sing, in a deep but slightly quavering voice, an old Romani song that it was to be my pleasure to hear sung in a multitude of different areas of Britain, under all sorts of conditions, over the course of the next sixty years, though I did not, of course, realise it then.

The song was 'The Romani Rai' – a lovely old melody, from generations past; humorous, sentimental, and optimistic, beloved by every Romani I have ever met.

The appearance of this ancient Romani man seemed to be beneficial to the spirits of everyone present, and singers, both men and women, young and old, needed little coaxing to take their places at the microphone.

To me the most fascinating and rewarding were those with 'out-door' voices, more used to singing in the open air around the wood fire. The clarity and simplicity of their songs, many old Romani ones that they had learned from their mothers, were very moving. Indeed, the respect with which those particular performers were received I found especially gratifying to behold. I began, after so short a time in their company, to appreciate the deep pride which they all had in their heritage. It was faintly ironic to find that the Romani people, in many instances despised and looked-down upon by the majority of *gaujo* (non-Romani) people, did, in truth, harbour those very feelings themselves toward their would-be oppressors — and not without cause!

By about nine o'clock all the beer had been drunk, and Bronco and Ike disappeared in a small van belonging to one of Bronco's brothers, to return in about half an hour with an imposing array of crates of ale which they off-loaded with some speed and stowed inside the house, ready for re-distribution to those present who were anxious not to dehydrate.

I myself had not yet begun to drink alcohol at all, so, perhaps rather feebly, I retained an intake purely restricted to orange juice. (In later years, however, orange juice, unless accompanied by a double measure of gin or vodka, never passed my lips!)

A little later in the evening a rather fine-looking man, in his early forties I guessed, with greying hair in tight ringlets, and sideburns, swarthy and almost Indian-looking, took to the microphone. His appearance caused a flutter of interest amongst the dancers and those seated round the room.

"Now we'll hear some singing, *mush* (man)," said Ike to me. "It's 'Frisco's Bill!"

"'Frisco's Bill?" I repeated, fascinated.

"*Owli* (yes). He's the best singer in this country; the dead-spit of Frank Sinatra, you see if he ain't!"

"The best singer among Travellers – on me mother's life," enthused Bonny, backing-up his brother's assertions with enthusiasm to be admired.

'Frisco's Bill was one of a kind of person who was usually, I gathered, liked or hated in equal amounts, mainly owing to his air of both contempt and egocentric self-confidence. His business was contained in the Reclamation of Metals industry, and by employing a certain whimsicality combined with ingenuity and imagination, he had succeeded in putting together sufficient wealth to enable him to reside in a large property on the outskirts of the town, drive a new limousine (when such were still virtually unobtainable just after the War) and send his two children to a private school. But he would still boast that he was born in a waggon on common land, could not read nor write, and was not deemed fit for National Service. Yet by perseverance and exploiting his personality, he was, without doubt, a millionaire.

On his father's side, he was related to Bronco by way of being a kind of second cousin – as was explained to me.

Despite his wealth and living conditions, however, he was to be much applauded for not abandoning his roots – never denying, in any way, his Romani blood.

Once on the microphone he seemed at once comfortable and relaxed. Immediately he commenced singing the floor fell quiet and murmurs of admiration could be heard.

His repertoire, seeming almost endless, of the songs of the famous crooner, were performed with a style and panache which many a professional would envy, leaving us stunned at his abilities.

As he finished each melody the walls of the little house seemed to shake under the resounding applause, which 'Frisco's' Bill received with gracious aplomb, gazing occasionally across towards his wife for her approval.

His wife, Mary-Janey, was a graceful if largely-built woman, her looks both striking and hard. She had the slightly haggard features that so often, I noticed, afflicted those who had been once-beautiful but whose lives had been filled with nerve-racking events which gradually fought their way out and into sight of all. Some might call them the faces of experience, or even of character: whatever it was it seemed unlikely that they would ever disappear.

Mary-Janey, Ike told me, was a niece of his grandmother, Aunt Kizzy, which is why her presence was expected. I noticed that, unlike almost all of the other women, she had abandoned the nearly universal hair-style of braids hanging loose, or coiled in a mountainous coifs on the tops of their head, in favour of a less dramatic and very non-Travellery short-styled 'perm.' As she was of rather heavy and unmistakeably Romani features, and the 'perm' was rather unattractive, I could not see it as an advantageous move – though I kept that opinion to myself!

Sitting beside Mary-Janey was her daughter Anne-Marie, a girl of about eighteen with long dark hair and enormous hoop gold earrings. She was wearing a dress of black satin which appeared a touch uneasy at the pressures that were being put on its seams. About her features played a slightly dissatisfied expression, and in her eyes was the look of the true predator. She was one of only two children, the other being a boy – maybe a year or so younger – 'Frisco's Bill's Bill, or as he was generally, apparently, called, Young 'Frisco.

The latter showed every indication, in appearance anyway, of being an exact replica of his father. He was, indeed, exerting a great magnetic charm upon all the unattached young women at the party, a fact of which he seemed fully aware. His was obviously to be the mixed blessing which invariably accompanies the fate of those who are exceptionally well endowed with a handsome exterior. For some it is their blessing, and others their undoing and a pathway to unhappiness.

To myself, alas, not feeling that I had such advantages in my youth, or even in middle age, my envy of such people seems never to have lessened.

I was lost amid such pondering when I was accosted by a middle-aged woman, yet another aunt of Ike's, who was known as 'Aunty Divvy Mary' owing to her severe complaint of religious mania. It seemed to be her life's work to attempt to foist her unremittingly fundamentalist beliefs on anyone unwary enough to be drawn into her company. Her husband, Ivor, had long since expired, driven, it was rumoured, demented by her preachings. She was left with one son, Jack, who was partially so afflicted and was referred to as 'Jesus Jack' – though not often to his face as he was known to 'turn' unexpectedly and deliver a powerful straight left to the face of anyone who offended him.

Aunt Mary, however, was in exceptionally good spirits that day, having won £500 at the races only a week previously.

When questioned about the moralities of backing horses in relation to her religious beliefs she was recorded as answering:

"If the dear Blessed Lord didn't want no horses to run then He wouldn't have made them!"

This reasoning was backed up by yet another, this one concerning the rights and wrongs of consuming alcohol.

"It's quite all right to drink," she asserted, reasoning, "The Dear Blessed Lord hisself always drunk up his wine."

Against such truisms none but the most foolhardy could argue, especially if Jesus Jack was in the vicinity.

All the foregoing had been told to me by Ike and Bonny, so I advisedly kept my conversation to the minimum.

The party's jollifications continued apace, an increase in sound becoming more and more evident, and features became a trifle more florid. At one point a minor disturbance was caused when Young Jobi and yet another cousin, Cock-eyed Jim, suddenly came together in a short but ferocious exchange of blows – the cause unknown to us. However, neither was viewed as being of much danger, and they were quietened-down without effort.

"Only bits of boys – nothin' to worry about," observed an especially striking-looking old man, dressed in a black yoke-backed jacket and knee breeches and brown boots. I was told that he was Old Tommy Skeeter from Poole in Dorset, the founder and owner of one of the first car-breaking yards ever established there.

Later I was introduced to him, and on my enquiring as to his health he smiled dolefully and replied:

"Well, young man, I ain't too bad seein' as how I'll be eighty-one next birthday. Fax the matter is, if I didn't have no water-troubles I'd be so good as new, thank the dear God."

His old wife, tiny, wrinkle-faced and wizened, sat beside him, almost lost in the luxuriance of a full-length black mink coat. It was a sight to gladden even the most lachrymose of persons, to witness the figures of the elegant old Aunt Kizzy and her friend Athalia Skeeter: their like will never be seen again, of that there is no doubt.

The party was much to the taste of Aunt Kizzy who, as the evening wore on, grew more and more merry, at length exclaiming loudly:

"H'I'm eighty year old an' I feels frisky as a two-year old! Fax is I shouldn't mind starting all over – if I could find meself a new man!"

Those nearby laughed appreciatively at her jests.

It was good to see her gleaming black eyes shining with mirth and pride in her family.

At that point she struggled to her feet and launched into an old Travellers' song, a ballad of some mournfulness, which reduced some of the women, especially the more senior, to tears. Indeed, at its close, it needed the vitality-filled figure of Aunt Rhody, another matriarch of some standing, to leap up and perform a lively song from the repertoire of Gracie Fields, for a change in mood toward the hysterical!

It was almost midnight when the guests began departing, apart from the two families with horse-drawn trolleys who had left at dusk. At a time when, according to one of the women, the light was beginning to fade and it was coming 'dimsy-dark' – description of twilight which forever caught my imagination.

Outside, the sound of staccato back-firings from unwilling-to-start engines disturbed the night air. The heavier engines of the lorries and vans were being subjected to mighty revving from their often inexperienced drivers, then to be left ticking-over whilst the passengers struggled up into the cabs, or if no room, then onto the backs of the lorries. The consequences of a wind-swept ride home held no fear for people with a lifetime's exposure to the open air.

Gradually, after screams and shouts of farewell to all and sundry, with special farewells to Aunt Kizzy, the narrow little road was emptied of all traffic.

"Come back in for a cup of tea, kid," invited Bronco, seeing me outside talking to Ike.

I declined his offer as I knew that I would be awakened in the morning by seven-thirty at the latest. Late rising was frowned upon by all in Queen's Park.

Thus I set off on my lone walk homewards, my mind filled with excitement at the events of the evening – even though I knew that to share them with my mother would have brought even further wrath upon my head. With luck she would not hear me quietly enter the house during the early hours.

By a quarter past one I was sound asleep and nobody the wiser.

Chapter Six

The Artist in Waiting

When I was sixteen, and perhaps but fourteen in any semblance of maturity, I managed to persuade my parents, in my on-going determination to avoid any form of regular employment, to allow me to enrol at the town's art school on the only course which they would consider: namely Commercial Art. The latter was a sure-fire ticket to failure for me, as I had no talent for lettering, and little for any other form of commercial art either. I was quite learned on matters of the History of Art, and of the Old Masters, the Impressionists, and many twentieth century artists too. (The last, needless to say, were heartily despised by our suburban neighbours, for many of whom the name Picasso was almost as disgusting as Hitler!)

However, as always, I ostensibly concurred with their wishes, and enrolled for four days a week. Privately, I felt confident that if I had managed to play truant successfully over a period of years whilst at school, it should not be difficult to follow suit in the notoriously lax atmosphere of such a college.

Reality proved such to be the case. The term started in September and we were in the middle of what used to be called an 'Indian Summer.' Hence very little of my time was spent indoors, and little or no attempt was made to absorb the intricacies of Commercial Art.

By that age my skills at shoplifting were verging on the professional and to my consistent pride I was never caught. I had one or two near misses in the field of apprehension, but on each occasion by either a deft turn of phrase, or even of foot, calamity was averted.

Fat Sid and Yvette had similarly remained safe from prosecution from the law and were still willing to accept almost all of my offerings. My friends Ike and Bonny, to whom I was careful to offer relatively 'safe' items, nothing too 'warm,' were an added assistance to my 'black' income.

I found books the easiest things to 'lift' – the shop-owners generally seemed to be of a trusting nature – but unless they were of obvious value, or 'collectable' it was difficult to dispose of them easily. They were certainly of no interest to Fat Sid or Ike.

As in most fields of endeavour, whether legal or otherwise, I later found myself tending to specialise. This specialisation was in the world of clothing. In those days shops, even large departmental store, were almost without exception, free from any form of surveillance apart from the eagle-eyes of patrolling shop walkers. However, as the latter were as easily discernible to the professional 'shopper' as was the average plain-clothes detective readily picked-out when 'shadowing' his target, they presented no obstacle to the initiated.

Although several youths offered to accompany me on these missions I felt happier working alone, and knew that my unaccompanied presence would not cause the interest that a pair would provoke.

As my skill improved I found myself removing items 'to order' – thus being sure of an immediate financial return.

I cannot help but feel that I helped improve the standards of sartorial elegance, during that period, of a large number of what would otherwise have been shabby residents, in an area of a dozen square miles or so.

I became adroit at the art of double-dressing, which is to say that I would secrete three suits into a changing cubicle, don one under my own suit, and emerge with two suits which I turned away for one reason or another; the same system worked for shirts, pullovers, and waistcoats. I even managed, over a space of time, to obtain numerous leather jackets, and even Crombie and camel overcoats. Leather jackets and those particular overcoats were greatly in favour amongst those who, in the evenings at any rate, fancied that their appearance in such garb could do little but enhance their reputations. In retrospect I can only conclude that my youthful and innocent-looking appearance was of invaluable assistance to my success.

I opened a Post Office Savings Account in a new name with no difficulty. Suspicion was not rampant then!

And as I careered thoughtlessly on towards my eighteenth birthday I found that I was wealthier than I ever imagined I could be. I had saved almost £500! (In those days that was a very considerable amount.)

My brains were not, however, functioning as they should have been. When I was called for a Medical Examination prior to conscription I passed it as A1 – to my disgust. How I had hoped for a spot on a lung, or any other complaint which would have prevented my passing. I thought of one of Ike's cousins, a large muscled-up youth of some sixteen stone, who had been refused on what seemed rather nebulous grounds: Grade Four, and yet he was able to work long hours every day in his uncle's Car-Breakers' yard.

My dubiousness as to the benefits of Service Life was further stirred by my encounter with The Major. It was to me, at that age of innocence in all but thieving, an alarming happening.

On one or more of the days each week when I was at the Art School I would take a trolley-bus home for lunch, usually at the same time. On one or two occasions I had noticed a rather distinguished-looking, ageing, Major – with 'Pay Corps' inscribed on his epaulettes. He glanced at me with some interest. I looked away: I sensed a feeling of foreboding.

Several bus-rides later I was not a little disturbed to find him seated beside me. In close proximity he appeared older and more debauched-looking than I had realised. There was about his well-modelled cadaverous features a theatrical and slightly unreal air. His eyes, hooded though deep set, were of an unusual shade of blue – darker than I had ever seen before. He radiated a certain menace. I was dressed in what I imagined to be suitable Art School attire – casual jacket of rebuffed check, and green corduroys.

"Are you a student?" enquired the Major without preamble. Adding rather ominously, "I've seen you on the bus before."

I replied with little enthusiasm: I had no wish to further our acquaintance.

My surprise therefore knew few bounds when I perceived the presence of his signet-ringed hand placed lightly on my thigh.

"I like your trousers," he smiled in what I presumed he thought to be a winning manner. "I love corduroys."

"Lots of people wear them," I replied coldly.

"I know they do," his answer was quiet and silky. "But they don't wear them for the reasons *we* do, do they?"

Slightly shocked by the tone of the conversation I merely grunted. However, in no way put off he continued:

"I've a lot of corduroy *trousers* and jackets, in all sorts of colours – if you'd like to come round one evening you could try some on ….."

I thought with some relief that I had placed my Service preference as RAF, not the Army. I staggered from the bus in some turmoil pondering on what may have been the fate of many a young boy-soldier who had taken his fancy. Ceasing my bus-rides I encountered the Major no more.

To make the foregoing of possibly greater significance, and as an example of the myriad coincidences, both good and bad, which afflict us all, I must leap forward at least thirty-five years to one summer's day in the early nineteen seventies. I was 'calling' house-to-house in a very opulent suburb to the West of Bournemouth, in which vast detached houses stood, most surrounded by their own spacious acreage of elaborate gardens.

I was engaged in the hawking of pre-packed bags of Organic Compost – an invaluable asset, I assured prospective buyers, in the production of even more luxuriant growth and floral abundance within their carefully tended estates. It was, when attended by vigorous and convincing salesmanship, a reasonable living for those not plagued by an all-consuming desire for security of income.

In any event, I remember that the morning had progressed quite well and that I was down to but a dozen bags left to sell. I set off up yet another long and lonely pathway from front door to front door. The house, a splendid edifice devoted to the spirit of the 1930s, was coloured a pale daffodil yellow, with white doors and window-frames. A small Mercedes convertible sat comfortably in its shadow – black and white, gleaming with polished pride. I looked with envy at it and deduced from the number plate's suffix letter that it was a 1966 model. Though about ten years old, its immaculate appearance suggested that it was brand new.

I rang the doorbell, as always, urgently though not *too* strongly – a lesson learnt from earlier days when I had the habit of giving three or four rings as the norm. However, on one occasion, having given my customary quartet of rings, the door was flung open by an irate and portly Jewish lady who demanded, her face alight with fury: "So, where's the fire? Where's the fire already? Clear off and don't bother me again." So saying, she slammed the door, and thus another little lesson in life was absorbed.

Now, the door was opened by a strikingly handsome old gentleman, his bald head was rescued at the sides and back by strands of thick white hair, curling yet tamed. His face was hawk like, a little marred by a profusion of carelessly distributed age-spots, and a pencil-thin moustache lay quietly between nose and upper lip.

He was clad in an arresting medley of tasteful and expensive fabrics, from his silk shirt and *foulard* tie, to his skilfully tailored suit of tweed woven in a subtle checked mixture of moss greens, His dandified appearance was assisted by the presence of chestnut coloured suede jodhpur boots of an opulent texture.

He was very amiable and responded well to my overtures. Indeed, I easily sold him the dozen bags – at what I might describe as a 'reasonable price.'

"Please call again if you are in the area," he suggested.

Delighted to have uncovered such an agreeable old man, I assured him that such would be my pleasure.

In fact, barely a fortnight later, I found myself in the neighbourhood when business matters were seemingly at a standstill. However, it not being my intention to deprive the compost of a new home, I sat pondering on where I might try, when suddenly I recollected the old man who had asked me to 'call again.'

No sooner had he come to mind than I was restored in spirit, and within minutes was speeding off in the direction of 'Green Tiles,' as the house was called.

The bell was soon answered by the old gentleman, as before, though on this day a strangely sinister figure lurked in the hallway, elegantly dressed, with obviously dyed black hair. The latter, like the fur of old tom cats, was flecked with streaks of reddish brown.

"Ah! It's that rogue again!" exclaimed the old man, placing a monocle stylishly to an eye.

The sinister one smiled fondly at him but offered me no sympathetic look.

After an easy transaction, disposing of all of the twenty bags on my lorry, I was about to leave when, removing his monocle the ancient man remarked:

"You're very smart – I like your trousers!"

Momentarily, I was taken aback, even though his cheque to me had been signed 'M. Mill-Burnside (Major, retired.)' Mixed feelings rushed through me. Strongest of all was my surprise in the fact that I was utterly charmed by this apparently fine old gentleman, with no signs of the repulsively predatory-gay that he had seemed to me when I was sixteen. My life and experiences began revolving before me with no solutions being offered. How sad it all seemed to me then.

Suffice to say, on thinking rapidly on the past, I found myself a solution. Some would find it an acceptable, private, form of revenge. Others would despise me.

It left me not *wholly* dissatisfied, with nobody actually hurt, and a *slight* recompense for an experience which many might have viewed as of no significance at all. Whilst others could sympathise with my feelings of uncertainty and horror which it had engendered. With the ability developed by the battle for survival, I managed to spin a convincing tale of need to the ancient military man, obtaining as a loan, a sum which I felt might be a small compensation for the unease which he had awakened in me all those years before. I did not, needless to say, have any intention of repaying it.

Chapter Seven

The Visit

 I had gradually formed a habit of going out on Sundays with either Ike or Bonny. If I met Bonny we were forced to ride our bicycles, take a bus, or walk. With Ike, however, our scope for travel was enlarged by reason of his motor vehicle. His latest possession was a very well-preserved Bedford lorry (a 30cwt – the Travellers' favourite) of 1947 vintage. It was painted a discreet maroon colour and lined-out with straw-coloured scrolls and a traditional buckle-belt design on each door, circular with the previous owners' initials within each. It had, of course, been a Travellers' motor. Petrol powered, with leather upholstery, it carried an unmistakeable and characteristic odour, peculiar to elderly commercial vehicles. It was Ike that I had intended to meet that Sunday, with the promise of going out into Dorset to visit a great Uncle and Aunt of his who were reported to be stopping with their waggons and horses some twenty miles distant in the direction of Shaftesbury, or maybe moved on to near Wimborne.

It was his Uncle Monty and Aunt Miella, the latter being a sister of his grandmother Aunt Kizzy. Some of their married children were stopping with them – six or seven waggons in all.

I had seen photographs of them on the walls in Ike's home, and was much looking forward actually to seeing them as they seemed extraordinarily picturesque.

I called round at Ike's at about eleven on the Sunday morning – Sunday being the approved day for visiting – and on arrival climbed up into the cab of the little lorry. Ike jumped up into the cab also and pulling out the choke, and jiggling his foot up and down on the accelerator-pedal – in defiance of engineers' recommendations – he nonetheless succeeded in starting up on the first pull of the starter button. To those who have ever owned or driven the early Bedfords the roar of the great six-cylinder engines will never be forgotten, nor the sweeping sound of its revs as one pulled away.

"Nice motor, Ike," I observed, knowing it would please him. Adding for good measure, "You can't beat a Bedford, eh?"

"I got this little motor off me Uncle Alf," he disclosed. "It ain't hardly done no work, 'cos he've been bad for the last two years an' he wouldn't let his boy drive it – 'cos he's too mad-headed."

"I've never seen a cleaner one, for its age," I said, with a smile.

The petrol gauge flickered on to 'half-full' so we were well set up for a longish journey, which was important as in those days the numbers of filling-stations were few, and those open on Sundays, fewer still.

"Let's hope we don't get pulled-up," said Ike," adding, "If I had a proper *slang* (licence) I shouldn't give a fuck – but you knows what some of them *gavvers* (police) is: they goes through everything if they thinks you'm Travellers. Bastards, some of 'em."

Although then innocent in such matters concerning our traffic constabulary, I was later to be frequently reminded of his comments.

Ike Pike's Bedford

"I don't know for sure whether me Aunt Miella's still over Shaftesbury Common or whether they've pulled over to Wimborne. Anyway we'll go over Wimborne way first an' if they *is atched* (stopped) there it'll save us goin' right over Shaftesbury way."

This seemed very wise to me, so we headed out to Ferndown and took the main road towards Wimborne. Within the area of Ferndown were several settlements of Travellers, in their own little communities, on land that they themselves had bought during the 1930s. Their accommodation was of great variety. Many had acquired old trailer caravans of differing sizes, others were living in old Romani waggons, and railway carriages. Others still had found that even ex-service glider aircraft shells could be converted into little homes, whilst the more prosperous had erected large huts or chalets in which they resided in comparative splendour. As is the Travellers' custom, most of the inhabitants in each settlement were related in some way.

Hence on our journey around Ferndown we encountered a number of obviously Travellers' motors, which resulted in much mutual waving and flashing of lights in greetings. It was a novel experience for me then. And yet again I was reminded of the fact that to be a Traveller is to be a member of a huge, but exclusive, club in which reputation and respect are to be cultivated; a largely secret world.

It was getting towards midday as we approached Wimborne, and, with the hunger of youth, we pulled-in to a lay-by beside an aged bus which had been converted into a café, enjoying the legend, 'Dinah's Diner,' displayed tastefully in the destination panel.

We locked the lorry doors and walked in to the 'Diner.' If its exterior bore the signs of hard-times and ill-usage then so did its interior bear them even more severely.

The atmosphere of general decay was very slightly remedied by the personable young woman who proved to be the owner. In her early thirties, with metallic-looking staring blonde hair of considerable length she did, in fact, slightly resemble Fat Sid's friend Yvette in form and colouration. Around her head was a kind of plastic Alice band.

"*Dordi* (Oh dear)!" murmured Ike, winking at me.

"Hello, lovey," greeted the young woman in an accent more reminiscent of Wigan Pier than that of Bournemouth Pier.

"Got any chips, darlin'?" asked Ike directly.

"Yeah," she replied.

"An' sausages?" he further enquired.

"Yeah," she replied.

"Let's have two lots an' two teas – needy style, okay?" he grinned. We seated ourselves, the only customers, and waited as our meals were being prepared.

"See that *rakli* (girl)," said Ike quietly. "She's a Traveller, or half one anyway, I'd bet me life. Did you see how she looked at us when I said 'needy'?"

By that time in his life he had left both Bonny and me far behind him in his experiences with girls.

Dinah's Diner

Like many young Traveller men, he was engaged in a fairly indiscriminate series of collisions with easy-going young *gauji* (non-Romani) girls before searching for a Romani girl to marry.

The fact that Ike was so spectacularly good looking greatly assisted him along his paths of seduction; in fact, he was becoming quite blasé about his affairs.

Glancing at the girl he remarked: "I could fuck that in two minutes – but I wouldn't touch it, on my life."

Once Ike had drawn my attention to it, I could easily discern a fleeting 'Traveller-look' about her features, combined with her independent manner.

After eating with great speed, we had soon devoured the wholesome refreshment offered by the sausages and chips.

"Look in again if you're this way, lovey," shouted the proprietor in husky tones, simpering at Ike.

"Yep, see you again, darling,'" called Ike, and we were off.

"She must be from North Country Travellers, judging by her speech," I observed, as we left, to seek out his relatives. Ike showed no interest.

"My Lord above," he exclaimed, "they're the most old-fashioned Travellers you could meet – all me Granny's people was the same, proper old-fashioned Romanies. Never have nothin' to do with *gaujes*, 'cept to get money off 'em."

"I hope we can find them," I said, of his relatives who we were seeking.

"We'll find 'em – even if we searches all day," Ike assured me.

"I ain't been this way since I come out here with me dad," Ike admitted, adding optimistically, "but I never forgets a road, kid."

As soon as we reached Wimborne we drove into the town centre and, after a few moments of indecision, Ike headed out on a minor road marked Holt Forest.

It was narrow but negotiable with care and after a couple of miles or so we found ourselves suddenly faced by a large green, about which were a dozen or more horses, mostly tethered on long 'plug' chains, whilst a few wandered free. The majority were coloured cobs all capable of pulling waggons. Aware, as ever, like dogs, of the presence of a Traveller-owned motor vehicle, they all raised their heads to scrutinize us. Several lurchers snaked out from the waggons, barking suspiciously. Behind them, in the lee of the forest itself, were six or seven waggons, mostly brightly-painted, though not smart. They were all, without exception, square-bowed, as opposed to being barrel-topped, the square-bow being especially favoured by Dorset and Wiltshire Travellers in that era. Later such a shape was virtually to disappear, the prettier Barrel-top taking over almost entirely, except, of course, for the few Reading, Showman-shaped, and Ledge Waggons still in existence.

To swing out from the narrow lane and be faced with such a sight was a picture to be harboured and treasured in the mind – certainly for me. It was the first time that I had ever been presented with such a scene, viewed from the standpoint of a visitor.

Within moments of the horses' heads being raised there issued forth a group of perhaps a dozen children, ranging in ages from about three to perhaps twelve or fourteen, girls and boys, and all dressed in ill-fitting hand-me-down clothes of clashing colours and designs: the detritus from the opulent suburbs in which their mothers had been 'calling.' As they drew closer some called out, "Uncle Ike – it's me, Uncle Ike!" in evident pleasure at recognising their visitor. Their little faces were sunburned and smoky, their hair matt, mostly blonde, and all hand-cut by inexpert barbers. Their Dickensian aspect was their charm. Without exception they all smiled a welcome.

By most of the waggons a fire was burning, some with black pots hanging from 'cranes' or 'kettle-irons,' with food in preparation. Others had burned down, smouldering until re-built again.

The day was sunny, though not too hot, and the adults were mainly sitting in small groups talking together. On the steps of one of the waggons was seated the figure of an extraordinarily weather beaten and worn-out looking man. His features were long and rather a pale yellowish brown, his nose uncommonly hooked, whilst his eyes were a gleaming black, like those of a field-mouse. On his head, brim down-turned, sat a faded green velour hat, from which at sides and back, there protruded tufts of thick white hair. Around his neck was a multi-coloured silk *diklo* (neckerchief), knotted gypsy-style. It was Uncle Monty, I gathered, as Ike made straight for him and addressed him with great respect: he was his grandmother's brother-in-law.

Just inside the waggon, seated on a stool smoking a bitten-down blackish clay pipe was an old woman the like of whom I had never before seen. Gnarled, wizened, toothless, her almost opaque pale blue eyes watering in the smoke from her pipe, yet piercing in their gaze, all added up to the formation of the stuff of which legends are made. One could not help but feel that their antiquity was such that their hold on to life was unlikely to have much future. Their lives had been filled with such hardship that anyone born after, say, 1950 would have been completely unable, even with the best will in the world, to comprehend even a quarter of the hardships which befell them *each week* during the course of their mishap-filled existence – persecuted and harassed in a manner undreamed of today.

The fact that they had relatives scattered all round at least four counties might well be understood better when one learned that old Monty was one of twenty-two children; and all twenty-two had survived and produced progeny of their own. Born under hedges, in bender tents, and in waggons, whatever, their survival rates were, considering, a tribute to the hardiness of their stock, and to their determination to do their best to prevent the gypsy-people from dying out!

Ike was able to fill-in the aged couple regarding his family, their relatives, and a few stories of 'scandalisation' which might offend their moral code, but which they apparently enjoyed hearing about.

As Ike was talking to the matriarch and patriarch several men and a few women, drifted around us, all smoking unceasingly on roll-ups of a remarkable spindliness, filled with the universally favoured 'Black Beauty' 'baccy,' of which I have written previously. It's sweet, yet insidious, fumes seemed to catch in my throat and larynx with some ill-effects, and I coughed unceasingly.

"My boy," said Aunt Miella, "you sounds like you'm branichal – an' I should know 'cos I bin sufferin' branchi-tees an' a mortified leg fer these past four years. I've a-bin underneath two doctors, an' the dear men cain't do nothin' fer me. 'Unluckiest complaint in the world,' one of 'em said to me. An' I sez 'God's cuss on whoever 'twas as gimme the fuckin' complaint in the first place!'"

This drew a mixture of reactions from the audience, many of whom, I fancied had heard it before. Nonetheless, owing to her seniority, and her rumoured association with witchcraft, she was given the respect which she felt was her due.

At that point our privacy was invaded by a small collection of bantam hens and one fearsome-looking little cock-bird. They appeared to be bearing down on the crouched form of a battered-seeming Gamecock which was tethered by a piece of baler-twine by one leg, under the waggon of the old couple. It rose, struggling, to its feet on sight of the bantams, ruffling its feathers and striking an antagonistic pose. However, before the bantams reached the waggon they were spotted by Aunt Miella who emitted a screech of fury, her wizened features contorted with rage.

"Gooo-aaan you fuckin' bastards!" she screamed at the little group of poultry. "God's cuss that cock-bird! He flew on me head an' crowed five times the other day. God's cuss that bird – 'twas he as brought that complaint on in me leg."

"Don't talk like that, Mother," urged one of her daughters, knowing that such upsets could not be beneficial to the old woman's health.

"I'll talk how I likes, my gal," pronounced Aunt Miella. "I knows this – 'tis the God A'mighty's truth!. That poxy-eyed bird brought back me complaint in me leg. If it hadn't bin for him I shoulda bin runnin' around like a young 'oman – not stuck yere like a poor old cripple-'oman."

Ike secretly winked at me, and we endeavoured to change the subject, which was difficult as Aunt Miella, like most of her relatives, was of a strong unswerving character and intent on drawing attention to the misfortunes which life had piled upon her through no fault of her own.

A few *gaujo* people sauntered by along the road, gazing in curiosity in our direction, on a Sunday stroll

At least four lurchers, rough-coated and of uncertain temper, sped out barking across the common.

They were only halted in their rush by a concerted cry from five or six men of:

"Go back dogs.......GOOO AN' LAY DOWN.......LAY DOWN...."

This had the desired affect and the chastened dogs slunk back beneath their respective waggons.

One of the men, yet another cousin of Ike's, drew to his attention that he had some puppies to sell.

"Come an' have a look, Ike," he coaxed, "They'm lovely puppies, all rough-coated. They come out've that bitch what Long Jim had off me uncle Black Siddy from Bath. You seen her run on Salisbury Downs when some of them Lees come over wi' their dogs. But not a one of 'em could beat that bitch – you must mind the time, eh, boy?"

"Yeah, I does," agreed Ike. "I come over wi' me dad an' Uncle Patch an' one of the back wheels come off the van half way through Warminster – you never seen nothin' like it. 'Tis a wonder we weren't all killed stone-dead, Tom."

"Come an' have a look at these puppies," urged the man, nodding at me to do likewise.

We walked past three waggons, all brightly painted and lived-in looking, with harness thrown on the ground beside them in most cases, though a few, more careful, had stowed in on canvas sheets under either the waggons or a trolley if they possessed one. Tom's waggon was painted blue and yellow, the under works and wheels 'lined-out' in red.

His wife, her black hair in long plaits, and dressed in a plaid skirt and old-style black 'pinna,' sat round a small fire with a babe-in-arms and two little boys.

"Hello, Ike – how's yer Mother?" she enquired, her voice low pitched.

"Hello, Carrie," replied Ike politely. "She's all right – fax they'm all all right thanks." Then, grinning broadly, he added, "How're you findin' the Romani life?" She had come from settled-down Travellers so the outdoor existence must have been a little unnerving.

"'Tis all right when the sun's shinin' an' you pulled in a nice place – but otherwise it's like its Granny!" she replied cheerfully. A light four-wheeled trolley was near to the waggon, with a sheet hanging down over its sides to afford some shelter to the bitch that was stationed beneath.

She was something of a deerhound cross greyhound, with maybe a touch of Salukie or Afghan Hound in her pedigree, tall and graceful and fast. Her colour was very dark, almost black: she was a very handsome animal. There were seven pups of which the majority had followed their mother in colouration whilst three were much lighter – one almost blue and two quite wheaten.

"I bet me dad would like one," mused Ike. "He always had a dog for runnin' up till two or three years ago."

"Gone too *gauji*fied (non-Romani-like), Bronco, since he took that job on the Council," laughed Tom, but with no malice

"What you askin' for 'em?" enquired Ike, casually.

Tom stared at him for a second before replying, his face emotionless:

"You'm can have your choice, except for that one big black bitch, at ten pounds for the dogs and twelve for the bitches, an' that's givin' 'em away, kid."

Who would have been able to imagine, in those far off days of the 1940s, that forward in the years following 2000 one would be asked eighty to one hundred pounds for even the most mixed breed of 'terrier' – rising into the hundreds for even the commonest of pedigreed breeds. At which one can only concede there to have been wisdom in the head of the street match-seller who observed: "Better to be able to buy a box of matches for fifty pence than *not* be able to buy a box for *one* penny!"

"I'd try to have a deal wi' you, Tom," observed Ike cautiously, adding: "But how about if me dad didn't want the puppy when I got him home – they ain't the easiest things, *jukes* (dogs), when you'm in a *kair* (house), you knows that."

"Pah!" rejoined Tom, raising his trilby hat and running his fingers through his matted hair. "Don't talk like a *dinilo* (fool), Ike. Why, a sensible man like you could sell un on in five minutes – an' take a nice bit of profit, like me dead Father."

With such an assault on both his pride and his capabilities I saw that Ike was almost cornered. However, he rallied slightly.

"No, I can't take one on – but I tell you what I will do: I'll risk me dad's buyin' him from me an' I'll give you seven pounds for a black dog puppy. How about that, Tom?"

Tom affected shock at such an offer, declining it forcefully in a tone that brooked no argument.

"You know what they say, Tom," continued Ike: "One bidder's worth a hundred lookers-on – ain't that right?"

"Not that kind of bidder ain't!"

It seemed to me that progress was not to be made, but, to my surprise, Tom appeared to return to a mood of greater reason.

"I tell you what I'll do," he said calmly. "Seein' as how your biddin' me, an' you're a long ways from home, I'll take one price an' one price only for a black pup – gimme nine pounds and take un on."

Ike gave him a level gaze, and, as ever when witnessing a Romani deal, my admiration for the two participants knew no bounds. Slowly, with repressed drama, Ike held out his hand, by now carried away in the excitement of the contest, and, his face tautened with determination, made his final bid:

"I've bid you Tom, an' now I'll bid you – this is me last bid, on me Mother's life. I'll give you eight pounds an' not one penny more, God strike me dead!"

The last was said with such force that it was obvious that he meant it. For a moment the deal hung in the balance, before Tom flung out his hand to slap the palm of Ike. The deal was done.

The puppy, which was reckoned to be about eight weeks old was put, slightly dazed-looking, in a cardboard box with the lids tied down – its future uncertain.

"Well, we'd better *jal* (go) on back I s'pose, Tom. I only hopes me dad'll pay me for the *juke*, said Ike," adding, "We'd best go an' say *tiro* (farewell) to the dear old people."

Old Monty was still seated on the waggon footboard puffing away on a small pipe which was smoking heavily, and not smelling entirely of Black Beauty. Old Monty, as was his habit in the name of economy, had introduced not only tea-leaves but tiny black embers from the *yog* (fire) in the creation of his own private smoking-mixture. Then approaching eighty years of age, such callous treatment of his lungs and chest did not appear to have wreaked much havoc.

"How long you stopping here, Uncle Monty?" enquired Ike.

"We'm goin' away in the morning,' young man," replied the old man. "The *gavvers* (police) come to us five minutes after we got here, an' they'm summonsing us if we don't shift first thing. Treatin' us wusser'n dogs they is, like me dead Father."

At this moment Aunt Miella appeared from inside the waggon, her ancient time and care worn features creased into a million wrinkles, her eyes twinkling, however.

"You'm off, then?" she observed. "Well when you gets home make sure as you gives my kind love to me dear sister – even tho' she'm half a witch!" she laughed.

And so, under the eyes of most of the adults, and all of the children, we stowed the puppy's box in the lorry cab and, climbing in, were soon bumping over the uneven green and onto the little road to Wimborne.

The little puppy uttered a few subdued whines, fearsome at what was happening.

"I hope he ain't gonna start howlin' all the way home," said Ike, undoubtedly a little concerned as to whether he had done the right thing in the matter of the purchase.

The light was beginning to fade as we drove through Wimborne and on towards Ferndown.

We had passed the lay-by, on which, closed for the night, the gloomy corpse of the converted bus sat mournfully in the twilight.

"So help me God, that *rakli* (girl) was half a Traveller," remarked Ike, his thoughts wandering back to our luncheon encounter.

We sped along, the little lorry's engine purring contentedly.

"She's runnin' sweet as a nut, ain't she, *mush* (man)," said Ike, obviously looking out for compliments – which, to my mind, he was perfectly entitled to do. Many of his relatives, some twice his age, possessed motor vehicles of such broken-down appearance and performance that they stood no comparison with his smart little Bedford. To be that successful whilst still so young promised much for the future. Youth, good looks, good brain, and endless ambition – what more could be desired?

It was all but dark when we reached Ike's home and as we pulled-up Bronco appeared at the door.

"Find 'em all right – is they at Wimborne?" he asked at once. He listened intently as we described our visit. His interest, so close was he still to the Old Life, that he demanded to know full details of the waggons, horses, and.....dogs. At the latter enquiry, Ike grinned sheepishly at him.

"I got somethin' here for you, Dad," said Ike, drawing Bronco over to the lorry cab and opening the box to show a rather mystified puppy.

Despite himself I could see that Bronco was pleasantly surprised.

"He ain't a bad pup," he admitted. "Whose bitch did he come out of?"

Having been apprised of all known details of the puppy's pedigree and price he seemed quite happy. And, even more importantly for Ike, he paid him without demur, retiring to the back yard in order to find accommodation for the new arrival. To almost all Travellers any young animal is given favour and succour: it is a pleasing characteristic.

"Well, me Dad seems to think the *juke* (dog) is *kushti* (good)," Ike remarked, with some relief.

At this we bade each other farewell, and I began my lonely journey back to Queen's Park. But my heart was with the glorious 'raggle-taggle' of the temporary residents at Holt Forest.

Chapter Eight

To Make a Man

It was on the January 1st of 1948 that there finally slipped through the letter-box of my home the dreaded command that I should report to RAF Padgate, near Warrington, Lancashire, for the pleasure of National Service (as it was euphemistically termed) for a period of two years. I had been out all day and my parents handed me the ominous-looking envelope on my return.

I received it with the kind of reaction generally associated with that of patients whose doctor has given them news of their terminal illness. It was then I fully realised the strength of my ability to dismiss unpleasant happenings from my mind, which I had done. The arrival of the distressing missive was, therefore, of a double shock in its impact on me.

I cannot recall exactly the length of the gap between the date of receiving the letter to the date on which I was ordered to appear as a recruit: I think it was but a week. I do remember the horror and trepidation which the proposed union between myself and the RAF caused me to feel.

As always, I took my troubles, in search of some comfort of a kind that I would not receive from my parents, to Ike and his family. For they, being sensible people, would, I knew, be in full sympathy with my distress.

Ike himself had, thus far, managed to avoid the degradation of being conscripted by the very simple device of not 'Registering,' as was legally required when one reached eighteen. (That was my first realisation that the art of fighting bureaucracy was, in fact, not to *confront* it – for thus there was no chance of bureaucracy's victory: more satisfying, was to take the secret way of avoiding all contact with it. Unfortunately for me my parents were too much in control in such matters for me to have followed that particular course.)

Ike's brother, Bonny, traversed an even more risky and hazardous path with surprising success. Accompanied by his father Bronco, he attended the Medical Examination which preceded 'grading' of recruits' mental and physical condition. Gone, however, was the smart and good-looking youth usually to be seen. In his place there was a shambling figure, hair unkempt, a tic in one eye, and an alarming grin of accentuated radiance playing about his features. He declined to speak, but uttered a series of disjointed giggles, I was told, and would not sit down – at one point attempting to climb up a curtain! His clothing was ill-fitting, his Norman Wisdom-like suit being two or three sizes too small. As had been planned, he completely ignored his father's admonitions and implorings regarding his conduct.

The doctors were slightly baffled, though they attempted to comfort his obviously distressed parent.

After brief consultation they placed him as Grade 4 – completely unacceptable for National Service.

By all accounts his performance was of such a high standard that, had an agent seen it, and had he himself so desired, his future in the acting profession would have been assured!

I was refreshed by his success, but it in no way lessened the impact of my own unhappy position.

During the actual War many Travellers served with distinction and bravery, whilst others ignored the whole thing – regarding themselves as being disconnected with what was, to them, a *gaujo* (non-Romani) matter only. I remember, a few years on, meeting a waggon and horse with a young Romani man leading them along an A-road near to Cambridge. I knew his family and had been told earlier that he was 'in the army' against his wishes or inclinations. He was known as 'Popeye,' for what reason I do not know.

"Out of the *culli* (army), then Popeye?" said I, stating the obvious.

"I wasted six months in there," he replied balefully. "But this is what I was waiting for."

He extracted from his pocket a rather greasy document and invited me to read it.

It was very official looking, with a variety of military insignia upon it.

It was the last line to which he pointed, with pride. *Dishonourably Discharged*, it read. Its effect as a tonic to the temperament of Popeye could not be denied. His unstable military service apparently mirrored that of the Kray Twins (those notorious victims of British injustice) being similar in many respects and with a comparable end-result. I felt pleased for him, and glad to see him back in a way of life to which he was eminently more suited.

Ike's complete family offered me sympathy and advice on my plight, their feelings and empathy again filling me with sorrow that my own parents remained entrenched in their stubborn assertion that the period ahead of me would achieve the curious attainment of 'Making a Man of me.'

Strangely enough I was quite happy as I was!

It is difficult to convey my feeling of utter despair on taking the train from Bournemouth; my Free Rail Pass and a small suitcase being all that accompanied me. It was the beginning of a journey the outcome of which was, I am fairly convinced, responsible for the whole pattern of my future – even if not apparent at that time.

The journey remains unclear, and un-retraceable until its culmination at the gates of the uninspiring and formidable entrance of RAF Padgate.

The full complement of that day's recruits was directed to one of the seemingly hundreds of almost identical Nissan Huts which lay in abundance, in neat rows, as far as one could see.

We were sectioned-off into groups of maybe twenty or so, mostly cowed and unsure of what was awaiting us. The hut to which we were sent was bare and Spartan inside; beds, free from the luxury of actual bedding, were placed along each wall, and in the centre of the building was a lone coal-burning stove resembling a barrel in shape and size, a glowing mass of red-hot coals throwing out a surprising heat from its open doors. As so often in life fire was the only comfort.

Eventually we were each provided with blankets and sheets and were ordered to make our beds. This was no great hardship to me as I had always made my own bed for as long as I could remember. For others though, used to the tender assistance in such daily chores by their affectionate mothers, the task seemed almost insurmountable. Having at last completed matters to the satisfaction of a low-ranking airman, we were directed to yet another hut wherein, we were assured, a goodly assortment of victuals awaited our pleasure. As ever chance provided me with a 'neighbour,' bed-wise, of an especially lowly order. He had, it transpired, journeyed all the way from Glasgow for this event. This came as no surprise once he spoke: his accent, guttural and sporadic, could only have been intelligible or appreciated by anyone, outside his neighbourhood, whose studies in dialects of Britain were extensive and all consuming. I was almost unable to understand a word he said and my need for constant requests for him to repeat his comments were something of an embarrassment to us both. I was particularly fascinated by his apparent need to expectorate on the hut's floor after every remark.

His name turned out to be Jimmy Batto, which I soon came to discover to be more interesting than its owner. Alas, chain-smoking and already married "wi' a wee bairn in the oven," he felt himself to be a man amongst boys.

An evening with the other occupants of 'me' hut, however, did not bring much return. Amongst a slightly greyish collection of youths only a cockney, who arrived in an American-style 'drape' suit, in pale gabardine, was very memorable. There was one other, a rather tall and pale youth of distinctly 'Queen's Park' aspect who sought out my company for a short while. However, after boasting of his scholastic achievements, of his School Certificate and of how he had "matriculated at fifteen," he was utterly contemptuous when I divulged my own lack of any achievements in the field of education. In fact, he was so disgusted that, thankfully, he refrained from any further contact with me unless absolutely unavoidable. He was quite soon, I learnt, recommended as being of 'officer material.' It was very depressing.

The next morning we were awoken early and escorted to yet another identical hut, from the exterior anyway, inside of which were numerous rows of counters piled high with heaps of brand new uniforms – jackets, trousers, shirts, boots and headgear – all awaiting fitting to our assorted sizes by rather indifferent-looking RAF personnel.

Although my brain may have been difficult to fit into any specific demography my physique was not unusual enough to demand any visit to the 'outsize' category of garments. Thus I was soon rigged-out, without drama or delay. Returning to our night-time hut we were ordered to don our respective uniforms, which we did with some self-consciousness. I was struck by the heaviness and the harshness of the uniform's fabric, especially the trousers, the weight of which made one grateful that it was not summer.

As one who had long favoured the languid comfort of suede or soft leather footwear I was greatly discomfited by both the weight and lack of any pliancy in the enormous cartoon-like objects we were expected to wear on our feet, and, worse still, clean with pride. There had to be more to life than such a numbing routine I thought, my mind running back over my years in Bournemouth, and the pleasures I had experienced in my own little world – above all its *freedom*.

At that moment I fully decided that Service Life was not for me. After all, by now the *war* was *over* – it had been *won*. There were no longer any enemies at the door. I was not eluding *active* service, I just wanted some of the *freedom* for which so many had fought. So it was a matter of urgency to me that I put plans into action.

Perhaps I should add that during the short space of time between receiving my Call-up Papers and my arrival in Lancashire I had devoted almost all of my time, except when visiting the Pike family, in a fulsome study in the Bournemouth Reference Library, of every book that I could lay my hands on that dealt with the subject of psychiatry and mental illness in general – for that, I decided, would be my only escape route.

It proved an enlightening source for study, and I soon discovered that the hazardous trek ahead must aim towards convincing the authorities that I was either a Manic Depressive *or* Schizophrenic. After lengthy studies of case-histories of sufferers from both ailments I decided that manic depression was my favourite, with perhaps a *hint* of schizophrenia thrown in by way of producing drawings of a bedazzling yet faintly demented nature. My confidence that I *could* produce such artwork was indeed proof that my short sojourn at the Art School had not been an entire waste of time – not that, by any stretch of the imagination, could my future creations be regarded as Commercial Art!

On the third morning after arrival I commenced the operation. Firstly I reported to the Medical Officer that I was unable to sleep *at all*, and was prescribed some phenol-barbitone tablets, detached from my group, and placed in a kind of semi Sick Bay "for a day or so," while my condition was investigated. This entailed a long interview with a young Medical Officer whom I found quite pleasant. However, despite personal feelings I knew it was of dire importance that I could convince him of my unhinged predilections. Typical of the times, much was made of my educational background – about which I romanticised wildly, hoping, and presuming, rightly as it happened, that they would not spare the time to check my scholastic history and its accuracy. Fortunately, given my fascination and accuracy for, mimicry, I had no difficulty in conducting all our interviews in the affected tones which were the hallmark of all graduates from public schools at that period in time. I had, in fact, concocted a complete fantasy regarding both my background and my schooling. In regards to the latter I assured the M.O. that I had enjoyed firstly private tuition and then been admitted to a small but distinguished public school. In retrospect it seems quite extraordinary that such easily verifiable fictions went unchecked. I explained that, owing to a youth plagued by ill-health and problems with my 'nerves' (a popular euphemism in those times for almost any form of mental shortcoming or disorder) I had emerged without any academic qualifications whatsoever.

Eventually, having apparently been slightly bemused by the events relayed to him he observed:

"Well, I think we'll keep you here for a day or so. Squadron Leader Austin returns from leave next week and I'd like him to have a word with you."

It was going well. The rest of my contingent had been passed on and were engaging in the notorious spell of unpleasantness known then as 'Square Bashing.' The latter exercise, as the nickname implies, was composed of the double-concentrations of marching in unison, up down and around in prescribed patterns – usually conducted by men with voices of phenomenal volume – for hours at a time. The rest of the time was spent in cleaning one's buttons and boots and all other equipment.

From observation I noted that these practices would appear to be nothing but detrimental to the physique and spirit of those taking part. The Authorities, of course, declared that their effect in instilling 'discipline' into even the most unwilling recruits, would prove to be of life-enhancing qualities and values in their future.

From *personal* experience, of course, I can neither confirm or deny the claim.

The ward in which I had been temporarily placed was a peculiar one, rather disorganised, and with a rapidly floating population, mainly much older than myself. Indeed as the weekend approached I was assured by one of its inhabitants that I would stand a very good chance of obtaining a 'Weekend Pass,' as there was no chance of my seeing the absent Squadron Leader until the following week.

Thus, cheered at the thought, I approached a sergeant whose job it was to issue such joyful documents, and it appeared that he was left to make his own judgement.

He listened to my request, drawing heavily and constantly on a Craven-A cigarette, enveloping both me and himself in clouds of smoke. Disregarding the perils that might beset one's lungs or heart, the manufacturer of that particular tobacco felt able to reassure one that, "for your throat's sake," it was advisable to choose their brand for inhalation.

"I can let you have a pass from Friday night at five o'clock till midnight on Sunday, OK chuck?"

My pleasure at this release, even for so short a duration, was uplifting in the extreme.

I was out of the main gates on Friday by one minute past five o'clock, making my way to the railway station. My journey would entail two changes of train and I could not expect to arrive at Bournemouth Central much before one a.m. The weather that January was dank and cold, though not comparable to the arctic conditions of the previous winter, and I huddled down in the carriage determining to keep a low profile for the journey. My first train left before half-past five, by a lucky chance, and my ease of connections for the rest of the journey would have brought comfort even to the most disillusioned of N.U.R. Members.

Arriving at Bournemouth I quickly decided that a taxi would be my speediest transport to Queen's Park, and so it proved. I approached our front door at 1.15.am. I had telephoned my parents and told them of my late arrival, requesting them not to wake up, promising to meet them at breakfast.

With an innate knowledge of how best to deal with them, I omitted to mention that I was in a semi-hospital ward. I merely told them that it was a 'normal' weekend pass.

Thus I found myself with all Saturday and about three-quarters of Sunday before my demanded return was due. How strange it was to be free – even if for so short a time.

At breakfast in the morning, after about six hours sleep, I found my parents both to be in reasonably amiable moods, like cats after drinking the cream. Undoubtedly they felt that they had, at last, won a battle with me. The question as to how happily, or otherwise, I was accepting the experience was not voiced. Happiness of mind had never taken first place on life's agenda, alas.

It is not that I am being purposely uncharitable to them out of spite, but, as one of nature's oddments, I never felt able or wished to follow the set patterns to which they had devoted themselves. It was almost as if my mother denied her past, and my father denied his future. It was not that I felt *superior*, just ill-fitting – as though my genes had taken a jump and landed clumsily.

Thus, after a fairly stilted conversation, I set off for the town centre, and found myself within the fineries of Bournemouth's only Lyons Tea Shop, situated in the Square. I was seated far inside and enjoying a pleasing cup of coffee and a cake, whilst glancing with interest at those lucky enough to be sharing my pleasure.

Lyons, as possibly one of its most admirable traits, appeared to draw an assortment of humanity, from the rich, the comfortably-off, the poor, and the down-and-out verge – plus a small number of striking eccentrics, again of all social spheres. All were patrons.

That morning one of the more extreme of the latter was present, nicknamed 'The Colonel.' He was a fine figure of a man, about 6ft 4ins, and of stalwart physique. He sported a heavy black beard beneath a woollen headgear which resembled a peaked tea-cosy. His unvarying apparel was a pale lightweight 'Desert' suit, belted, with matching shorts. His sturdy calves were warmed by knitted woollen stockings in the top of which lurked two matching dirks. Polished brogues completed his garb. He generally slung a haversack about his shoulders but sometimes, as the mood took him I presume, he suspended two or three swords and daggers from his belt in a blatant way, which would have caused convulsions had he been observed by a present-day member of the Health and Safety Brigade!

The revelation that he was a member of a West Country land-owning family of immense wealth and power, could have contributed to the fact that he seemed to remain un-accosted by authority. He habitually rode, at high speed about the town, on a large-framed bicycle, with 28″ wheels – the sort once favoured by enthusiastic and athletic village constables. He was a solitary figure, and I never saw him in conversation with anyone. Living alone in a block of luxury flats his seemed a lonely, though maybe happy, life.

Another curiosity, rather less fortunate than 'The Colonel,' was a horrifyingly contorted and malformed woman of incalculable age; permanently shaking, all her horrifically twisted limbs, she proceeded about the town with great regularity, wrapping herself, and her independently moving limbs, about the frame of an all wooden folding pushchair of an age near to that of an antique. Her name, inappropriately and slightly tragically, was reputed to be Daphne Pugh – though, again, I never witnessed her in conversation. In Lyons, she seemed always to remain in isolation, tucked far into a corner by herself.

A lady from the upper echelons would occasionally deign to enter accompanied by a minute Pomeranian dog which she thrust into a fur handbag when inside the café. I was fascinated by her apparel, especially in winter when she was always swathed in an opulent fur coat draped about her corpulent form. Despite this amplitude, however, minutely thin little legs emerged at the hem of the coat, with tiny feet encased in high-heeled footwear.

I was reminded of her many years later when an old Traveller whom I knew was denouncing the skeletal stature of a woman of his acquaintance. "God strike me dead," he had exclaimed. "If she was to *chop* legs wi' a sparrow that bird'd get the worst of the deal!"

Her distinguished features were a trifle debauched by time and over-indulgences, but were compensated by her fine white hair, worn with great style in a kind of hirsute tower, almost a foot in height. Bejewelled and bedecked she must surely have stirred the imaginations of any aging romantic from the age of fifty onwards. Her like would seem to be a rare sight today.

There was also, as a regular patron, an especially unattractive and tubby little woman, about whose raddled features there still played a self-confidence which hinted at a lively past. Her hair was thinning slightly, after a lifetime's over-enthusiastic applications of exciting colorants one could but assume.

During that time, in the summer, the National Coal Board, in a fit of humanitarianism, had formed a branch which spent its time in despatching groups of worn-down coal miners from South Wales to Bournemouth for a week or two to recuperate. I am not sure whether the aim was to condition them in order that they might enjoy a well-earned retirement, or whether it was intended that the short break within the Bournemouth sea-air ridden beaches would ensure their return to sufficient good health to enable them to renew their hitherto mole-like burrowings.

In any event, easily-recognisable in their dark blue suits, white scarves, and black caps, these worthy sons of toil would, without fail, find their way into Lyons on their way to the sea-shore. The past attractions of the blonde lady, and still eloquently displayed as a hint of past excesses, proved too much for those little, lustfully disposed, Welshmen to resist. With extraordinary regularity and enthusiasm they would gather at her table, offering her a splendid and generous supply of Lyons Swiss Roll as a forerunner to suggestions of a more personal nature. She was the elderly ex-goodtime girl, still activating hearts and minds without difficulty.

One of my last memories of her is an event of some curiosity which took place on the beach itself on a sunny day in summer. I was seated on the sand, gazing out across the sea in the direction of Swanage when I became aware of a chorus of singing drawing nearing to me from the direction of the promenade. I realised, upon sighting a group of dark-suited figures, rather short of stature, accompanied by a lone golden-haired, and rotund, little woman, what was causing the not unpleasant sound. From the slightly off-key nature of the song, combined with a universal unsteadiness of stride, it took no great feat of brain-power to deduce the degree of their alcohol-induced good cheer.

However, my astonishment increased as they approached the sea-shore itself, led by the little woman's encouraging cries, and proceeded, fully clad in their best suits, to stride into the waves with utter abandon, stumbling and choking with a mixture of sea-water and laughter.

The sight was too much for me and I withdrew towards the promenade, my last sight being of one swamped-looking woman, hair awash and her floral imitation-silk dress clinging affectionately to her generous curves, surrounded by a dozen or more little black-capped figures bobbing up and down in abandoned bliss.

The rarity value of such a scene has remained with me for ever: its like probably never to be witnessed again!

After this interlude I left the seafront and took a bus in the direction of Ike's home. It being a Saturday afternoon I knew they were likely to be within its precincts. Even the self-employed Ike did not work through the weekends.

I passed the shop of Fat Sid and Yvette as I walked, of necessity, through back-streets, there being no bus routes passing along such narrow thoroughfares.

Fat Sid happened to be at the shop doorway so I stopped, more out of politeness than love.

"Ain't seen you lately, cock," said Sid, lighting a small cigar. Yvette was visible inside the dark little shop, her clothes, as usual, more suggestive of a provincial and ambitious *soubrette* than a shop-owner. She waved non-committally on catching sight of me; her finger-nails I noted, were pure milk-white and tastefully polished. I explained to Fat Sid my unfortunate predicament.

"Fuckin' hell!" he exclaimed, one of his chins shaking in sympathy with another. "I never even knew you was eighteen. How did they come to catch you?" I thought you was too fly for that, cock."

"So did I," I replied, with the wisdom of afterthought.

"Here, Yve," he shouted back into the recesses behind him. "Fuck me if he ain't in the army – how about that?"

Yvette emerged, her white face entrancingly decorated in the image of a B-film leading lady, her long hair looping in a controlled style over one shoulder. I had rarely seen anyone so beautiful I thought.

"How're they treatin' you, darlin'?" she enquired, to my surprise.

"Better than I'm treating *them*!" I rejoined, causing her to smile encouragingly, and Fat Sid to bare his teeth and spit, with poor aim, at the gutter.

"We shan't see you for a while then, cock," observed Sid, the sun playing havoc with his already defective perspiration glands.

"Who knows – we may all get a surprise," I said, surprising myself.

"Hear that, Yve?" smiled Sid, picking up on the remark. "You can bet a hundred pounds he's gonna try an' work his ticket, ain't that right, cock?"

"I wish I could," I answered, more heartfelt than I sounded.

"Oh well, best of luck – an' don't fuck anything I wouldn't, cock!"

At which, and after a faintly simpering smile from the exciting Yvette, I continued my journey.

I pondered, imaginatively, on the charms of Yvette and felt slightly troubled as I realised that, late by many standards, my interest in girls – or more often *women* – was becoming a matter of greater importance in my life: I seemed to find myself, like a young John Betjeman, falling in love almost every day. It was becoming very trying.

As I neared Ike's house I perceived his little red lorry parked outside, and was cheered by the sight.

Bronco opened the door, a small roll-up Black Beauty in his mouth.

"Nice to see you, kid," he welcomed me warmly, adding, "Go on through. The boys is out the back."

Passing through the kitchen I exchanged a few words with Aunt Kizzy, who was, as usual, crouched in front of small wood fire in the grate, she too enjoying a similar roll-up to that of Bronco.

I told her of my dislike of Service Life and she expressed much sympathy for my plight.

"Like me dead Father, you'm gettin' more like a Traveller every time I sees you. You shouldn't be in them huts, 'ong've all them old *gaujes* (non-Romanies)," she asserted. "It ain't no life fer a Traveller, so help me God."

"I know," I replied. "But I'm going to try and get out."

"I'm glad to hear it," said she. "But 't'ain't no good you *prasterin'* (running away) from the *culli* (army) – 'cos iffen they 'kotches' you they'll lock you up in one o' they houses of glass – wusser'n prisons, be all accounts."

I reassured her on that point, but did not disclose my plans as such.

In the back yard I was pleased to see Ike and Bonny, with their cousin Black Boy and his girlfriend, a very dark complexioned member of the Lee family, and still on the roads. Her name, perhaps surprisingly, was Mary Lou – not that she and I spoke, her attention being fully occupied with the charms of Black Boy, whose colour, as his name suggested, matched her own. They made a handsome pair: I had only encountered Black Boy once before and had no reason not to like him.

"What's its like in the *culli, mush*?" enquired Ike, laughing quietly, adding slyly: "What've I missed? – not to mention the *dinilo* (fool) there." He grinned and laughed again, pointing at Bonny whose status had grown amongst the discerning, including myself, since his achievement at the medical examination.

I told them of the fictitious physical placing of Max Bacon as 2f 2f – and we all agreed that a similar grading must assuredly have been given to Fat Sid had he been in that situation.

"Fat Sid!" exclaimed Ike. "They'd have to get up early in the morning to catch him! Fly-est old *chavi* (boy) this side of Poole."

"I wouldn't mind his *rackli* (girl) though," enthused Bonny. "I definitely wouldn't throw her out've bed!"

"There's a boy," said Ike in mock reproof and the conversation changed.

Bonny made us all some tea, his mother and father had gone shopping, and we chattered on happily for an hour or so. I half promised them that I would meet them on Sunday morning to 'look at' some ponies, one of which Ike was thinking of buying so that he could enter into the Travellers' sport of trotting-horse racing which was becoming increasingly popular.

I hoped to go with them on Sunday, but had yet to find out whether or not my parents had made any arrangements for me elsewhere. Not very likely, I thought.

My parents seemed perfectly agreeable to my 'going out' on Sunday morning, upon my reassurances that I would be back by three o'clock at the latest, in order to catch the trains back to the horrors awaiting me.

Thus I arrived at Ike's before the eleven o'clock deadline which we had agreed, and after which time they would proceed without me. It seems strange today that one could be out of contact even if only a few miles apart – long before the magic of mobile 'phones, to which Travellers have taken like ducks to water.

The weather was an acceptable mixture of winter sunshine and light clouds, with almost a faint hint of spring in the air. Ike and Bonny were both seated in the cab of the spruced-up little lorry, with its radiator cap shining in the pale sunlight. During the week Ike had negotiated with a local blacksmith who had made an elongated vee-shaped tow bar – thus, to the initiated, destroying any slight notion that it might not be a Traveller's vehicle. The latter drawbar design was later to be superseded by the infinitely sturdier 'step-bar' which was both more practical and more impressive in appearance.

"He won't *jal* (go) back to no *culli* tonight," Bonny laughed. Adding mischievously: "He'll *praster* (run), on me mother's life!"

We all laughed, though I was, in truth, much taken by the idea. I felt, however, that it would be wiser to see how my own secret plans worked out before chancing 'desertion' and risking the severe punishment that I was warned of by Aunt Kizzy.

"Where are we going?" I asked in curiosity.

"Over to see me Uncle Siddy," Ike replied. "Me granny's youngest brother – he's got a bit of a place over agin Wareham, don't you know."

"How many ponies has he got?" I enquired.

"Dunno, do you?" replied Ike, looking at Bonny.

"Nah!" said Bonny. "You knows me Uncle Siddy – he haves more *grais* (horses) than I gets hot dinners."

"*Dordi* (oh dear)," grinned Ike. "Dear old *mush* must be seventy years old too. A proper old dealing-man, an' always has bin, be all

- 82 -

accounts. Me granny said he bought his first pony when he was on'y eight year old!"

Ike Pike, Smartly Dressed

"I tell you what, tho,'" added Bonny comfortingly. "You wouldn't get nothin' bad poked into you if he knowed you – he keeps all the bad uns for the knackermen, or someone he've fell out with!"

We decided to go via Wimborne, and as we passed the familiar motor-coach café we decided to stop for a snack.

"Here, Bonny," said Ike. "See this *rackli* (girl) in here – well, she's a Traveller, you *dik* (see) and listen to her *rokker* (talk). If she ain't a Traveller then I'll pay for all three of us."

Our curiosity aroused, Bonny and I followed Ike into the shabby, yet clean, 'café.' A second, and closer, inspection of the young woman convinced me that there was no likelihood of Ike having to pay for the food for us all.

Her face brightened on seeing us enter, her attention focused on the most handsome of the three, namely Ike.

After an order of three 'sausage, bacon, egg, toast and tea,' which she received gracefully, Ike proceeded at once on to what could have been thin ice.

"No harm, darling," he began, "but you're a Traveller, ain't you – I can *dik* (see) it in your *yoks* (eyes); I'm right, ain't I?"

"'Course I am, love," she replied, her cold eyes lighting up momentarily at the admission.

"Who are you one of, then?" pressed Ike.

"Me dad was a Skeets," she answered, giving a local settled-down Travellers' family name.

"Anything to do with dear old Pincher?" enquired Ike.

"Yeah, sure," she replied. "He was me dad's oldest brother."

There followed an exchange of family names and relationships, which seemed to prove the old adage: One Traveller Knows Every Traveller. A not entirely exaggerated statement – and one which has proved an unending source of fascination during a lifetime's association with these wonderful, and unfairly denigrated, people who still cling to values long since deserted by the bulk of humanity in the Western World.

Great must be the comfort for Travellers, constantly and unexpectedly to run across others, all over the country, who on investigation prove to be relatives, even if quite distant. For the itinerant, in a world full of strangers, the feeling of loneliness can, at least to some extent, be slightly alleviated by these encounters. To one who has lived as and with Travellers for all of my adult life it has been of unending fascination to discover self-confessed Travellers living their lives alongside *gaujes* (non-Romanies), often in smart houses, and with the requisite new BMW cars, yet remaining slightly separate and aloof within the framework of their own success. It is, to my mind, a parallel that can be drawn with no other members of society apart from Jewish people – a race which has possibly suffered even more persecution and prejudice than the Romanies.

After our conversation became more personal and our origins had come out into the open, we all became more relaxed, unfettered by secrecy.

The young woman, Janey Skeets, insisted on treating us to a mug of tea apiece, and expressed the fond hope that we would call in again.

I could see why. The two handsome brothers, it being a Sunday, were attired in their best new suits. The latter were tailor-made, of dark and lustrous fabric, in the Traveller-style of that time favoured by the younger men. No longer were the heavy Derby-tweed suits of the older generation chosen, with their rows of stitches around the jacket edgings, and the old 'fall-front' trousers with 'leg of mutton' shaped legs. Those heavy tweeds, moleskin, the rarer 'owd dog,' or Derby covert cloth, were fast being abandoned for the slicker and lighter-weight clothing which was faintly influenced by the garments of certain Hollywood B-film actors. Jackets were rather square of cut, with pleats and yokes, and usually featured patch-pockets with button-down flaps; whilst the trousers were cut wide with a heavily raised seam down each leg. Some of the more adventurous even boasted the new and rather untried 'zip-fly' – regarded as somewhat daring by most tailors.

Both Ike and Bonny wore coloured neckerchiefs which were still in vogue – to be largely abandoned within a few years, except by the middle-aged and elderly. They were seen as being 'too Travellery' by the young.

Funnily enough, the Travellers' fancy for yellow or tan elastic-sided boots, jodhpur boots to give them their correct name, endured and were greatly liked by Travellers – and were to remain their favourite form of footwear for decades to come. Alas, however, eventually they too were dismissed for the same reason as the *diklo* (neckerchief) and gradually virtually disappeared.

I myself had donned my dark and rather '*gaujified*' (non- Romani-like) suit, and brown suede boots – which rather unadventurous apparel I had attempted to brighten up by the presence of a multi-coloured paisley silk scarf around my neck. It was faintly symbolic, and proved to my companions that I was not ashamed to be in their company nor of being taken as part of it: Travellers in those times were sensitive of the views of the average *gaujo* – a viewpoint of *gaujes* usually based on utterly false assumptions, and almost complete ignorance of the people who they had taken upon themselves to disdain. You were either *with* Travellers or against them, it seemed.

In any event, refreshed and somewhat cheered by our encounter we climbed back into the lorry cab and the little Bedford fired up at the first pull on the self-starter. Listening for a moment to its silky ticking-over even Bonny and myself, although both utter strangers to the complications of the petrol-engine, could appreciate the smoothness of the sound issuing forth. With a few revs Ike let in the clutch and, possibly more by luck than skill, effected the changes from first to second, then third gear: a matter of timing and experience as the gear-box was of the old 'crash' sort. Failure could result from the mistiming of the complicated operation known as 'double de-clutching,' from which , if discommoding, even the sturdiest of engines could suffer the equivalent of a human heart-attack.

However, Ike was a 'natural' driver hence his enthusiasm for machinery; and his delight in his new-found mobility, guided him optimistically through whatever obstacle fate placed in his path – youth and ambition were their own reward.

We soon reached the outskirts of the little Dorset town of Wareham, branching off the main highway on to a narrower, more rural-looking road. It being a Sunday, plus the fact that petrol was still rationed, combined also with the fact that 'austerity' ruled the country, were greatly responsible for the almost empty state of all the roads of motor traffic. As soon as we left the main road we overtook a rather genteel couple in a governess cart, their pony trotting sedately out towards the open country, then two lone cyclists, and nobody else.

We drove on for a mile or two and passed a semi-derelict double-decker bus on a rough kind of lay-by, from whence it had obviously not ventured forth for many months, if not years. Obviously it was now a family home. Its exterior, dark green and matt, was still graced by the faded and peeling remnants of several almost indecipherable one-time advertisements that had once been set before the travelling public. I was just able to discern the legend, "WINCARNIS WINE – FORTIFIES THE OVER FORTIES," the remains of the advertisement still clinging along one side. Disintegrating curtains hung from the windows and four or five small children, ragged and tow-headed played on broken tricycles and a scooter around its entrance door. As we drove by a gaunt black-haired woman stuck her head out of a window, wondering who we were. She waved slightly, and gazed non-committally at us. Ike gave a toot on the horn, but we did not stop.

"That's Two-thumbs Albert's gal who runned-off with Wisdom Leacock's boy," vouchsafed Ike, in tones of some disapproval.

"Cah!" exclaimed Bonny in equal disgust. "Was that the *mort* ('woman')? He must a-bin *dinilo* (foolish). Him a smart young fellow no more'n twenty." He added with some exaggeration, "That was the h'ugliest woman I've seen for years. On my life she must a-bin fifty years old!"

"I wouldn't stop – for no money," Ike assured us primly. "I'd as soon not speak to people like that."

We fell silent, pondering on the follies of man.

"How much further is it?" I asked, to break the silence.

"No more'n two mile, is it Ike?" replied Bonny

"Nah," said Ike.

About five minutes later he slowed down, and, without warning, turned in off the road on to a rough and un-made lane. Hoof-prints and iron-bonded wheel tracks were visible on the muddy surface, and after a couple of hundred yards we were confronted by a high corrugated-iron fence with two large gates for entry into the property. Visibility to the outside was screened by a profusion of untended Leylandi bushes, some of which were twenty feet in height. It was the end of the track so it was difficult to comprehend what might lay in readiness for our inspection – or at least for mine and Bonny's, Ike having been there many times before. He stopped the lorry across the gates and began sounding its klaxon-like horn in impatient blasts.

"Dear old *mush*," explained Ike. "He's deaf as a gatepost. If no one else is home we'll have to toot an' holler for two hours 'fore he hears us!" At which statement I realised that it might take up to five minutes before our calls were answered. Exaggeration in any form always, to my mind, adds energy and excitement to a conversation – among Travellers anyway.

Occasional bursts of barking could be heard, and some muffled cries of, "lay-down, dog. Bide quiet!"

"That's my Uncle Siddy – I heard him hollerin' at the *jukes* (dogs). He'll be down to let us in sharply," announced Ike with much confidence. Sure enough, very soon the barking of a dog grew closer behind the fence and there was a rattling of chains, combined with much coughing and cursing as the padlocks were unlocked.

Eventually the gate was opened a little and the features of the ancient Old Siddy were revealed – to me for the first time. His was a striking and incredibly old-fashioned figure. His face, dark brown, was lined to a degree that would have cast shame upon the late W.H Auden the poet. (About the latter someone is reputed to have observed: if his *face* is like that then what must his *scrotum* be like?) Old Siddy's eyes were glittering and almost black, unfortunately slightly crossed, both watering generously, flowing in little rivulets down his cheeks.

Clad in a well-worn black suit of heavy tweed and run-down black jodhpur boots, with a black and white spotted neckerchief and a hammered-down velour hat of a greenish-brown colouration, his was an arresting medley of both Romani and equine motifs. The likelihood of his being mistaken for a retired member of the Prudential Insurance Company was distinctly unlikely.

"Hello, Uncle Siddy, how are you keeping?" asked both of the boys politely.

"Well, I ain't too bad my boys," declared their great uncle, without much conviction. Adding as an affected afterthought: "If I never had no water-troubles an' I weren't fucked-up wi' the screws I reckon I'd be so good as new."

We all stood smiling at that revelation, and he beckoned us in.

"Leave that motor out there," he directed. "He'll be so safe as houses – no one don't come up here 'less I knows 'em." On that assurance we followed him inside, his old whippet-lurcher sniffing around us uncertainly with quiet growls and grumblings.

"She won't hurt you, not so long as I'm here," murmured Uncle Siddy, coughing bronchially and lighting a thin roll-up.

"These old fags'll kill me, iffen old-age don't do it first," he grinned. Adding, to my surprise: "Me dear old mother's a hundred next birthday an' smokes like a fuckin' chimbley. She'd sooner have her baccy than eat a bit of bread an' meat. She'll be up directly, you boys, so you best go in an' *rokker* (talk) to her, otherwise she'll be upset."

We walked along the track inside the gates, through some bushes and then, suddenly, the extent of Old Siddy's adventurous mixture of dwellings, stables, and sheds was revealed.

The most pleasing to me was Old Siddy's delightfully picturesque little wooden bungalow, minute by today's standards, but perfectly adequate for the accommodation of one or two persons. Gabled, with a spacious verandah along its frontage, and painted in maroon and straw-colour it was a tribute to the aesthetic eye of whoever built it. Alongside it, nearby, was a square-bowed 'Dorset' Open-lot waggon of a sadly distressed condition. The original paintwork hard to determine, its wooden wheels collapsing, no longer roadworthy. This was the last home of Old Siddy's aged mother and, as she was then ninety-nine her future was of a certainty limited. She had become something of a living legend, having in her time produced twenty children – most of whom were still alive, all in their seventies and eighties. Old Siddy was her eldest child, who she had produced some eighty years before!

Besides Old Siddy's bungalow and his mother's waggon there was a smartly maintained hut of some eight feet by twelve feet, with a small platform of decking across its frontage, upon which sat a set of folding chairs. Finished in black and white paint, with neatly pinned-back lace curtains and patterned roller-blinds, it was about the measurements of a suburban garage. A tall chimney extended upwards from the roof. In

Old Siddy

fact, the picturesque little construction provided a more than adequate home for Old Siddy's widowed daughter Lavinia and her young son Jobi, a boy of about ten or twelve. Pin-neat and cosy inside it had great charm. Lavinia herself, widowed when her man fell out of a tree whilst 'lopping' in suburbia, was of a fast disappearing image. Proud of her heritage she clung to the old ways of hair-style and dress. She was wearing a plaid skirt, dark blouse, and embroidered black 'pinna'; and her dark hair was long and braided, partially covered by a patterned head-scarf.

"Me dear old mother loved 'old-fashioneds' an' so does I too," she declared when I rather shyly complimented her on the quality of her appearance.

"Cah! She'm too old-fashioned!" declared the boy Jobi, grinning and adroitly dodging a poorly-aimed blow at his head, by Lavinia in pretended annoyance.

Besides these dwellings there was, partly-hidden by a huge pile of logs, a small, round, 'bender' (or 'rod') tent of a design still favoured, after hundreds of years, by very old-style Travellers – though often not from choice. Although there was a time, I am told, when many Travellers preferred to sleep on the ground rather than up in waggons. The tent, I learned, was inhabited by a single Traveller of late middle-age called Skylark. He was a brother of Old Siddy's late wife and thus was able to stay there whenever he felt the need. Otherwise he could be found, usually alone and hidden away, in many remote parts of Dorset or Somerset. When he returned, after an hour or so, I saw him to be a man rather small and squat, his hair grey and longish, his face flat and heavily lined. At first glance he appeared to be completely matt from head to toe: his features and his clothes showed no evidence of a concerted fight-back against the destructive effects of over-proximity to wood-smoke. He proved, however, perhaps owing to a lack of self-confidence, to be one of those rare souls who radiate such natural good manners and amiability that they arouse little or no animosity in whatever company they find themselves.

Needing very little money to maintain his frugal existence he was able to support himself without too much effort, performing any kind of menial task that he was offered, and even, when the mood took him, reverting to his gypsy ways, sitting before his stick fire engaged in making pegs. Indeed his production was spectacular, I was told, and for him to undertake the making of a gross of pegs within hours was no strain upon him, and his placidity remained unruffled.

Perhaps, to the uninitiated, only the presence of an iron 'crane', a black kettle, and a Travellers'-style hoop-handled frying pan beside the remains of a wood fire, would have raised their suspicion that they were beside someone's dwelling.

As well as this variety of homes, there was an assortment of horse-drawn carts and four-wheeled trolleys, upon some of which sets of harness were carelessly thrown.

Like all old-style Romani stopping-places there was about it an air of both transience and permanence. One somehow felt that everything, no matter how permanent looking, could easily disappear in a matter of hours. (A lifetime later I have never failed to be astounded at the speedy manner, having decided to move, that the Travellers can pack-up, hitch-on, and be gone – leaving little or nothing to show that their presence had ever existed there. Not that I am blind to the fact that *some* Travellers leave the ground in a condition that none but a refuse-tip manager could applaud. But they are, in fact, greatly in the minority, despite the falsehood so often concocted by the lower end of the tabloid press.) In any event I found the property of Old Siddy, and its occupants, to be immensely pleasurable.

Making Pegs

Old Siddy ushered us into his bungalow and we sat in the small kitchen whilst he made us some tea.

"Young Siddy is comin' over directly an' we can go an' look at they ponies," said Old Siddy, referring to his son who apparently lived not too far distant on a piece of land that he had bought and on which he had erected an imposing sectional chalet which his father described in reverential awe:

"My Siddy've bought hisself a lovely home," he assured us. "'Tis one o' they sexual bungalows – good enough for a *rai* (gentleman) so help me, Bob!"

At that moment we heard some rather unmusical notes coming from the gates, and the old lurcher jumped up, swaying slightly, emitting four or five strangulated barks.

"Goo an' lay down – God's cuss that dog!" cried Old Siddy, rather ungratefully. "That'll be my Siddy, I can take an oath on that!"

We gulped down the rest of our tea and made for the gates to meet Young Siddy. There was a careworn old motor van, hand-painted in chocolate brown with red wheels, about twenty years old, parked outside. Its dents and scrapes and other damage being worn without repair: it had suffered a rough passage. Standing beside it were two small men. The first, I deduced, was Young Siddy – his smoke-dulled face creased in a thousand wrinkles – who smiled in appreciation of his aged father and the smartly-turned out figures of Ike and Bonny, his dark eyes resting on me for just a second. Traveller-style he accepted that if I was with his two relatives then I must be 'all right.'

"Let's goo down an' look at they ponies," suggested Old Siddy, continuing: "These two boys might be in the mind for a bit o' trade. So let's sii if we got something they wants."

"Sure enough," agreed Young Siddy. "'Tain't far to where they'm to – we can walk there easy."

His accompanying friend remained totally wordless.

He was, it transpired, an orphan and only half a Traveller. Known as either The Friendless Boy or Chinese Jim he was reputed to be slightly sub-normal. However, he was strong and willing and spent his life willingly as a kind of slave, moving from one family to another and back again! Several Traveller girls of rather low brain-power had, I was told, flirted with him but it had come to nought. Their wariness of him was in no way diminished once they realised that for him to drink as little as half a pint of beer was enough to transform him into a homicidal maniac. Indeed, his offers to fight *anyone,* no matter what their pugilistic skills, struck awe and caution in the hearts of all but the most seasoned of fighting-men.

"You all right, my Jim?" enquired Old Siddy solicitously.

"Yes, fank you, Uncle Siddy," replied Jim, his eyes darting wildly in all directions, in overcoming shyness. To the best of my memory he did not utter another word. We came to a small and sheltered field in which about a dozen horses were grazing.

On hearing our voices, recognising they belonged to Travellers, all dozen raised their heads and stared at us fixedly without movement.

"There's a pretty pony, Ike," said Young Siddy, pointing to a rather fine-boned skewbald mare not far from us.

"She ain't too bad, *mush*," admitted Ike. "Have she bin in?"

"We had her in that trolley over there last week," said Siddy. "Ain't that right, Dad?"

"Ar," confirmed Old Siddy, mopping at his streaming eyes with a spotted handkerchief. "When she'm proper broke-in I can warranty she'll go like a greyhound dog, on me dear old mother's life."

"'I'll come over in a week or two an' see how she'm going,'" said Ike, noncommittally.

We surveyed the rest of the horses, although in my case I was, at that stage, no judge – though I might presume that something of my late grandfather's love and knowledge of them may perhaps have filtered through, to be later developed to some degree.

After an hour or so we agreed that we would come back in a fortnight, by which time Young Siddy assured Ike that the pony in which he had affected mild interest would be ready to be driven and handled 'by a baby.' It was, perhaps, sad to realise that such forms of enthusiastic salesmanship are rarely found today, in which such deals were conducted in a spirit of adventure combined with the skills of a poker-player. They were battles of both knowledge and wills, often taking many hours to fulfil, frequently lubricated towards their climax by the consumption of much alcohol, and further goaded by the encouragement of numerous bystanders, caught up helplessly in the magic rites of 'the deal.'

Old Siddy's daughter Lavinia generously offered to give us a helping of 'meat pudding' which she had prepared, cloth-encased, old-fashioned style, on a large stick fire outside her little home.

As is often the case with Travellers when 'visiting,' the two boys were 'ashamed' to accept actual food from their hosts, though drinks of tea were never refused.

And so, with hand-shakes and many wishes of goodwill to Ike's family from Old Siddy, Young Siddy, and the daughter, we left. Sadly the ancient matriarch was still asleep and Old Siddy felt it best not to waken her lest the excitement of seeing so many visitors might have brought on one of her 'turns.' The latter, apparently, were increasing in regularity and they inevitably felt that the end was near. I had been shown some photographs of the centenarian and was astounded. Swathed in a thick turban-like headdress, she sat crouched before an outdoor fire, glaring from gnarled and wizened features with, even though hostile-looking, the curious detached expression that so often seems to haunt the faces of the very aged. I would dearly have liked to see her seated beside Old Siddy, the twenty or so years age gap having been rendered negligible by time. Alas, it was something which I never did witness as her sojourn in this world ended but a week or so later.

The journey homewards seemed to pass with incredible rapidity, the approaching train-journey and its destination doing little to raise my spirits, which were lowering by the minute. I found myself gazing wordlessly out from the lorry's windows at the beautiful Dorset countryside as we sped along. I even pondered, without much conviction, whether I would myself one day own a lorry, and even manage to earn my living Traveller-style, working for myself and avoiding the terrifying drudgery of a nine-to-five existence which, to my never-ending astonishment, was accepted without question by the sons and daughters of the denizens of Queen's Park – and indeed almost everyone else – except Travellers, of course. Both Ike and Bonny, sensitive to my feelings, endeavoured to offer me words of advice and encouragement.

"You won't be in there long – take my word for that," said Ike encouragingly.

Bonny similarly expressed such thoughts and we parted amicably whilst voicing our hopes that we would meet again soon.

I was at home in time to snatch a cup of tea and some of my mother's 'lardy' cake, before setting off for the station and my train to purgatory.

Chapter Nine

Coming and Going

Within the anonymity of my RAF uniform, overcoat collar raised against the cold wind which had sprung up, it was not long before I was sitting mournfully in the first of the two trains which I had to negotiate for the journey northwards.

My spirits were not improved when, in the railway station while awaiting the arrival of my second train, I was standing by a cigarette-vending machine when a very supercilious young army officer hailed me in his most imperious tones:

"You there! Airman! Take your hands out of your pockets! Who do you think you are? How long have you been in the service?"

He fired several further questions at me, his expression becoming more and more contemptuous as he received my answers. The fact that all I was apparently guilty of was actually to have had my hands in my pockets, on a cold railway platform seemed to beggar belief at the treatment I was receiving.

It seemed that he was taking an unreasonable view of a trivial situation in my eyes, even if not in his own. After much lecturing and considerable pomposity from one so young he finally dismissed me, with dire warning as to my future in the armed forces.

It did nothing but reinforce my already determined belief that to avoid any form of Authority would henceforth be my premier aim. As things were it seemed that I was about to be forced into enduring a virtual prison sentence without any trial. I had, until that moment, tried unceasingly to be master of my own fate, and indeed had, until then, in my own mind, succeeded to a surprising degree.

I was in the position in which I found myself just then largely due to my ability to distance myself from events actually happening to me. In a sense, I realise now, I had developed a kind of theatrical personality but, tragically, had not then quite found the role to which I was best suited. My delight in living out those fantasies in my personal life was both an advantage and a handicap. Advantageous in the sense of knowing no responsibility for my role as suave and innocent-looking shoplifter, confident enough to feel certain that there was no chance that I would ever be apprehended, which was more or less true.

I would also tend regularly to develop various differing traits, usually trying to place myself as a person of social superiority in dress and mannerisms. Unhappily, if the truth were known, my life became an un-scripted play. But, without doubt, these traits were of unending assistance in the days ahead.

Upon returning to the RAF base, just before the time on my 'pass' expired, I found some confusion in picking-out the hut in which I was billeted from the hundreds of others of identical appearance. However, luck and desperation (two of the most rewarding of human conditions, I was later in life to discover) guided me safely into the gloomy ward.

I was soon abed whereupon a nursing orderly immediately issued me with a sleeping-pill which soon had the desired effect.

Early the next morning we were woken with the news that "The Squadron Leader is back from leave and will be conducting his rounds at nine o'clock."

The name of Squadron Leader Austin was spoken in hushed tones – apparently in psychiatric circles only the names of Jung or Freud evoked greater awe.

Eventually the hour drew nigh and our gloomy collection of humanity, the majority of whom displayed little or no indication of their inner turmoil which must, by their very presence in such a 'holding' ward, have been regarded as demanding investigation. Promptly at nine o'clock the door was opened and in strode a tall and distinguished-looking man of commanding presence, followed by another lesser officer and a Flight-Sergeant. (The latter, I discovered, were a breed apart, some indeed with temperaments which one felt could only have benefited from a session in which they themselves were confined to the psychiatrist's couch!)

The Squadron Leader had, of course, already spoken to many of the prospective patients before. Hence he devoted most of his time to those of us who were part of a fresh intake.

One unfortunate denizen, with an obviously middle-class background, whose brains were completely addled, demanded to know the business of the Squadron Leader, to the astonishment of all.

"Who am I?" answered the medical man, "Donald Duck!"

Dissatisfied with this reply, the disturbed airman flung himself down on his bed and dissolved into racking sobs.

Was this the standard psychiatric reply to those who questioned his qualification, I wondered. I had not uncovered its use in any of the 'case histories' that I had studied so intently in the Bournemouth Reference Library some weeks before.

After cursory remarks to those on my left side he gradually drew level with me.

"And how can we help you?" he enquired, the faint glimmer of a smile flickering across his face.

"Well, sir," I began, knowing that my fate hung in the balance. "I am not able to sleep *at all*," I said with emphasis, "and if I *do*, I get such terrible dreams that I feel I am going to die. But I am so depressed that I don't really care. In fact, I have saved up a lot of sleeping tablets and I think I'll ...."

"Stop there!" demanded the Squadron Leader. "I want to see you again – we'll try to fit you in later today."

So saying he continued his round.

I was left in something of a quandary, not sure whether I was on the way to achieving my goal or not. Time would tell, I comforted myself.

After the Squadron Leader had left the ward we were abandoned, more or less free to do what we liked. There was, of course, in those days no television to assist in the passing of time so all that was left was conversation, board-games, or letter-writing.

The latter was my choice. I felt that I should communicate with my mother and father, though not to apprise them of my actual true situation. It was a strange moment as I had never before penned *any* letter to my mother, and only a few very stilted notes to my father when he was in 'Kiss-land.'

It was not long before the orderlies arrived with trolleys of food, of a distinctly higher quality than was served to those suffering the unending drudgery of Basic Training, I was told – not having actual experience of that particular ritualised torture myself.

Barely had I finished my appetising desert of warm rice pudding and tinned pears when I was accosted by a Sergeant who ordered me to accompany him to the psychiatrist's lair.

I will not bore the reader with the details of the ensuing interview with the Squadron Leader. Sufficient to say that my performance must have at least equalled that of my role as Charlie Chan's Number One Son in the bygone school play as the upshot was:

"Well, I've got a kind heart, so we'll get you into hospital today, over near Bridgenorth. Get your things together and report to the Ambulance Bay in half an hour."

With that it was at an end, and the determining of my future lay within my own hands: a good performance, I realised, would bring more than applause – it would achieve Freedom!

I hastened back to the hut and gathered together my few belongings in a half-full kitbag. Well directed questions resulted in my path to the Ambulance Bay undergoing no complications and I was there, waiting, at the requisite time.

Various nursing staff questioned me and after a short while I was led towards a rather battered-looking RAF Ambulance of Wartime vintage, possibly of American origin.

The single rear door was opened and I was ushered inside. Within, to my surprise, I found myself confronted by a singularly unattractive-looking youth of about nineteen, in a crumpled uniform, hatless and tie-less. His hair, shorn to regulation severity, was of purest corn-colour; it was his only redeeming feature. The door was slammed shut and the two of us were locked-in together: I was instinctively grasped with unease. I sat down on one of the side-bunks in the rackety vehicle as it started-up and began moving towards our destination – a town of which its geographical location was something of a mystery to me. My nerves were slightly curdled and I was finding it difficult to comprehend fully the undoubted risks that I was undertaking, not that I could alter the situation. The youth sat quite still, his almost opaque grey eyes fixed upon me giving no definite clues, at that point, as to his well-being or otherwise.

"Where's you stationed to?" he eventually enquired in a broad accent which I was able to recognise as belonging to Plymouth. "Tryin' to work your ticket?" he asked, gazing coldly at me.

Innocent that I was in those days in such matters I immediately confirmed that that was indeed my aim.

Alas, it transpired, I could not have given a worse answer. The youth revealed, perhaps a little too tragically, that he was the victim of severe epilepsy and that he had already been discharged from the Royal Navy as being unfit for service. For reasons of his own, however, and with admirable optimism, he had immediately enrolled in the RAF without disclosing his ailment or his former brush with the naval authorities. However, as his seizures were of such a distressing nature, and liable to beset him at not infrequent intervals, he was at that moment being dispatched to the same hospital as myself. There was an irony in the situation: he *was* ill, and was deeply unhappy that he was about to be discharged as unfit; whilst I was his complete opposite!

After such a possibly unwise exchange of confidences we both pondered silently, the powerful engine of the ambulance affording us but little solace.

We remained thus for perhaps half and hour when suddenly, and with no warning that I had noticed, the youth became convulsed in what I realised must be a violent fit. Falling to the floor, his body assumed a number of unnatural-looking poses, and his whole frame shook as with a kind of palsy, whilst bubbles of foam emanated from his mouth. It was the first time that I had ever witnessed such a dramatic condition – far worse that that of the semi-torpid victims of air-raids whom I had seen being dug out and transferred to ambulances a few years before. I jumped up and knocked on the thick partition which separated us from the driver, hammering upon it in an effort to draw attention to his plight.

Alas, despite all my efforts, the driver and his colleague, both regular serving RAF personnel, failed to acknowledge that anything was wrong – or possibly they did not care. Who can tell? Thus I was left alone with the terrifying sight of the convulsing and contorted youth who, for all I knew, was about to expire. In fact, after a while he subsided into a kind of coma, seeming all but to retreat completely from his body.

It was in that state that he was discovered not long afterwards when we arrived at the air-base hospital. Two or three orderlies rushed into the vehicle and did their best to revive him.

"Looks like he's had his fucking chips," pronounced one of them with immediate medical diagnosis, and impressive indifference. They questioned me, but I felt it best to withhold any sensible replies.

I never encountered the youth again, so I am not able to state if he lived or whether the orderly had been correct. It was, as they say, 'water under the bridge' for me.

I was soon installed in the ward which had been chosen for me. Upon entering it I was immediately aware of the difference of its occupants to those of my previous 'holding' ward. Here, few could deny, I was plunged into the genuine 'loony bin' (as it was referred to by the jocular, if insensitive, of the era).

The first thing that struck me, apart from the physical appearance of most of the patients, was the fact that they were all wearing the regulation hospital uniform. The latter consisted of vivid almost cornflower-blue suits, white shirts, and bright pink ties. These garments, to me, were a distinct improvement on my previous garb. There were about twelve or fifteen patients there at the time, and a very mixed collection were they. One or two were suspended, heals higher than heads, in their beds, undergoing, I learnt, a treatment known as 'lumbar puncture,' in which fluid was drawn off, for a number of reasons which might prove beneficial to the condition of those who underwent it,

By and large, however, time proved them to be, generally speaking, a not unpleasant group of men, varying in age from about eighteen to their late thirties.

It was presumed, as a rule, that the older long-serving patients were undoubtedly under the weight of numerous psychological traumas and were genuine sufferers. The younger ones, it seemed, were regarded with a certain suspicion: the more eccentric their behaviour the more likely was their forcible return to active duty. On my second day there, as an example, I was approached by a pale-faced young man of maybe twenty years old, who asked me if I would write a letter to his home for him. Racked with suffering, whether real or assumed, his hands were so tremulous that he was unable to perform the act of writing legible correspondence. Conversation with him convinced me that his was genuinely a case in which he should surely have been given the benefit of any doubt. His whole condition was such that none but the most cynical medical man could have considered him fit for service. But, alas, after only a few days this unfortunate young man was cast from the hospital having been declared to be in A.1. health. (At that stage my confidence in my own future was badly shaken!)

Another man, of possibly twenty-five years old, a heavily-built and rather overweight native of a remote part of Lancashire, nicknamed 'Flash,' was in the next bed to me. Chattering incessantly, peering through round spectacles at a world which was rapidly becoming incomprehensible to him, his similarity in mannerisms to the average Pantomime Dame was undeniable. Unhappily he was in the grip of some form of malady which was causing him to regress, at an alarming rate, to a state of childhood – apparently finally to shuffle off this mortal coil with the mentality and aptitude of a tiny baby! His days, in every way, were numbered.

Others, with serious mental problems, sat unmoving in their chairs all day, nodding and muttering to themselves at intervals, quite impervious to the world around them.

But worse were the paranoid schizophrenics, whose wild delusions and sudden changes of mood, frequently ended-up in some form of violence, directed at anyone at hand or even against themselves. To an eighteen years old man, prospective Raffles of the shoplifting brotherhood, 'dealing man,' and hopefully future 'ladies' man' – but otherwise quite innocent of the world – the whole atmosphere seemed, in my somewhat shattered state, like something from a Breughel painting. Alarming, it most definitely was.

However, the universe is small and anything can happen. So it was that on my second day in residence a new patient arrived. Aged thirty to thirty-five, with sergeant's stripes on his uniform, I could sense that he was of a more interesting nature than any of the other patients. Showing no sign whatsoever of any form of illness he was of a strikingly handsome appearance, even flaunting a strangely swooping moustache and hair a little in excess of the regulation shearing. By chance there was an empty bed next to mine so he was allotted it to my delight.

His name was Francis Johannes, it emerged, and, to our mutual surprise, he had parents in Bournemouth where he had lived throughout his schooldays until joining-up in the hopes of becoming a pilot. The latter ambition, however, was precluded when he failed the eye-test. He had thence become a bandsman, rising to the dizzy heights of sergeant – but apparently, true to a trait evinced by certain upper-class men of that era, he refused the suggestion of 'officer training.' He preferred his lowlier ranking and its accompanying advantages of less responsibility, or so he told me later. His reasons were possibly not entirely divorced from the ones that caused Lawrence of Arabia himself to spend his last years as a low-ranking member of the RAF, seeking maybe, the need of anonymity – or was that, perhaps, just a romantic conjecture on my part? I will never know.

It appeared, from what he told me that he had been afflicted by bouts of severe depression of late, and it had been decided that hospitalisation for a short duration might, indeed, effect a cure for his ailment.

I noticed that he was a chain-smoker, and maybe a little withdrawn, but other than that he *appeared* to be in perfect health.

Being ranked as a sergeant he was afforded a greater degree of leniency from petty restrictions by the staff. Among the privileges which he enjoyed was permission to take afternoon walks outside the perimeter of the actual camp itself, being allowed a leave of up to four hours. It was to his great credit that, having struck up a friendship with me, he managed to persuade the ward staff that he would be responsible for me if I was allowed to accompany him.

I had by then been a patient for almost a week and, apart from brief consultations with three different doctors, nothing seemed to be happening as regards my treatment.

Just before the arrival of Francis, my only friend, I had been working on charcoal drawings in a small sketch-pad which I had brought with me. My memories of the Munche-like drawings I had seen when studying the literature on psychological problems and ailments, within the precincts of the Bournemouth County Reference Library, were still quite clear in my mind. Thus I set about endeavouring to produce my own, in an effort to prove that although the Age of Romance was said to be faltering, the Age of Imagination might still flourish.

I believe that my finest and most awe-inspiring drawing was an effort that intended to portray the condition of 'Frustration' in its most acute form.

I recollect that I produced the image of an infant, of indeterminate sex, lying on its back in a cradle, with legs and hands stretching upwards. The drama lay in the fact that neither the legs nor the arms were equipped with their appropriate hands or feet. In their place were little branches and tiny bunches of grapes, the latter hanging enticingly over the mouth of the baby – but just out of reach, and seemingly inaccessible to the open-mouthed infant! Its representation in black and red charcoal was, it must be admitted, jarring in its impact.

Others – Schizophrenia, Manic Depression, and even Senility, all were drawn, and each, had a macabre feeling about them, I hoped.

In fact, I was awoken at about 1.30 am one night and told I was to be interviewed by a 'new' psychiatrist. It was a favourite habit to call patients in the middle of the night – it was presumed that the spirit of malingerers would be at a low ebb, and that any attempts at deception as to their true states of mind would more easily be detected.

I was somewhat agitated to discern, on entering, that the doctor in front of me was no less than a comfortably matron-like lady, a WAAF officer of high rank.

For some reason, of chance intuition, I had brought my book of drawings with me for the interview. After several questions as to my judgement of my own state, which I managed to parry with only sporadic flirtations with the truth, I offered her my lurid depictions. Her reaction was better than I could have imagined. She gazed at them in wrapt attention, just now and then raising her eyes to peer fixedly at me with an expression very difficult to decipher.

After a few minutes she picked up her telephone and I heard her request someone at the end of the line to join her if possible. A minute or so later a rather elderly, bald-headed, stooping officer entered. He glanced at me with the minimum of interest and sat down beside the WAAF officer. They both lit cigarettes and studied my drawings without addressing me at all.

"I think we'd like to keep these, and show them to somebody else," she finally remarked, offering no hint as to their future or asking my permission to take them.

To my disgust it was the last I saw of them. I suppose I may derive a kind of ironic satisfaction as to their possible final resting place. Could they, to this very day, over sixty years later reside in a mouldering RAF archive? An example, one hopes, to current students of psychiatry, of the impenetrable mental ailments suffered by an unstable recruit circa 1948!

Days followed days – no hint of the secret workings within the medical world. My routine followed an almost set pattern. It consisted of lazy mornings, refreshed by snacks of food during the hours between nine and midday, after which I was nourished even further by the splendid choices offered at lunchtime. Once devoured, Francis and I would pursue our walks in the surrounding countryside, in an area of considerable natural beauty.

I did not apprise him of my multi-social entanglements or of my nefarious dealings before entering the RAF. I felt it wiser, and more understandable for him, to nest within my persona of Decent Young Englishman of Public School background. It was, I presumed, the wiser step. Notwithstanding that small concealment, I found our hours together rewarding and fulfilling, and I believe it was mutual. He was probably the only person in my life with whom I took long walks with entirely innocent motives: it was my last flush of childhood.

I had been almost two weeks in the ward, seeing a number of 'specialists' in various fields of psychiatry. By a series of miracles I had managed to forego the very dubious benefits of either Electric Shock treatment or the painful lumbar puncture.

Left alone for a few minutes at one of the interviews I had furtively stolen a glimpse into the doctor's notes on case histories, finally discovering my own name – at the end of which was written the unsure opinion: 'Man. Dep.' 'or Schiz?' Heartened though I was to observe the legend 'Man. Dep.' (which I took to be a short version of 'Manic Depression') I was much less comforted by the word 'Schiz.' From my studies in the library I had realised the horrific implications of such a dangerous illness. At all costs, I reminded myself, I must avoid the folly of suggesting that I was ever visited by the sound of 'voices' or accosted by figures from 'another world.' It was most certainly my intention to stick to gloom and mournfulness: in those circumstances not too difficult to manufacture.

My thoughts on the period in question, apart from any moral issues involved, from a distance of time, were largely of surprise at my own enterprise and determination. I should perhaps also stress that it was during a very strange time in history: as I mentioned earlier, we had won the war, mortal enemies at the time were non-existent, and all that everyone desired was to reap the results of our victory. Alas, however, food rationing continued for another nine years, and the whole of society seemed grey and gloomy.

It was not until the 1960s that – for a wonderful though brief span of years – people actually *enjoyed* the flippancies and trivialities of life in a glorious outburst of colour and abandonment. It was at least some part of the Freedom for which, legend hand it, our fathers had fought.

But, of course, killjoys, religious leaders, and, worst of all, politicians, all combined to put a stop to that. How could anyone have imagined that the denizens of this planet had actually been designed to *enjoy* themselves unless in a strictly controlled atmosphere of regimentation? Bogus moralities, as ever in our history, prevailed.

I was soon back in the ward, my only comfort being derived from conversation with my friend Francis, whose wisdom and experience I came to value acutely. It was he who informed me of the slow-moving machinations entailed in the study of each and every patient. His estimate of at least two more weeks, making four weeks spent in the ward, proved to be correct.

He told me, again correctly, that a 'Board' would have to study my psychiatric report, and that they would invariably accept its recommendations. My trepidation grew, therefore, when the next day I was given the time of my appointment with such a 'Board'. It was to be at 2pm.

I arrived at the door of the requisite office with the name of a Wing Commander affixed above it, at exactly the stated time, and knocking rather restrainedly on the door I managed to pick up a scarcely audible order of: 'Come.'

Upon entering I was confronted by an officer of considerable rank, his white-flecked moustache, somewhat nicotine-stained, hurtling out enthusiastically from each side of his nose; a curiosity of its time. His hair, also grey and white, was brushed sharply back from his forehead, flattened without mercy.

"Sit down," he said, to my surprise. "I have the doctors' report in front of me and I must ask you a few questions."

He thereupon commenced to interrogate me on almost all aspects of my life, both before and during my brief service with the RAF. I answered them as best I could, maintaining as far as I was able an expression of extreme dejection.

Suddenly, he looked hard at me and enquired, "And if we should recommend your discharge, then would you mind if we put down on your papers that you are a raving lunatic?" (Such, of course, would have rendered any employment quite impossible to find.) Momentarily taken aback though I was, I was nevertheless quick to assure him that it did not trouble me at all.

I could only believe that if I had objected to such a comment then it would surely have pointed towards a deception on my part. It seemed apparent to me that a genuine 'Man. Dep.' or even a 'Schiz.' would have been utterly indifferent in such a matter. It was probably a wise move.

After more cursory questions, and a short lecture on the enormous advantages of a spell in the Services, he finally dismissed me. I seemed, in my own mind, to be at a crossroads – I was dizzy with trepidation as to how matters would proceed.

My delight can really never be re-captured when, two days later, I was informed that my dismissal from the RAF had been achieved. I was graded 'Temperamentally unsuited to service *life*!' I could scarcely believe it, and my impatience to be home and *free* was almost immeasurable. On my last night I seemed to be afflicted by a mild form of 'gate fever' – that neurotic state which is said to attack prisoners, after a long jail sentence, on their last few hours before release.

My friend Francis was unreservedly thankful at my good news, expressing the hope that we might fix on a meeting in Bournemouth on his next leave. Alas, for a number of complicated reasons, it was a meeting that never materialised, and I never saw him again. It was sad, though possibly not a senseless decision. I felt that, meeting as we did in an island of semi-lunacy, amidst *other* situations we would probably later endeavour to forget. It was, I felt, fate that drew us together, and fate that later kept us apart.

Chapter Ten

Free Again

M_y collection of relief document, discharge papers, and a variety of official papers were received by myself in something akin to a state of coma. Even the fact that I had been classed as 'Temperamentally unsuited to Service Life' did not then fully enter my consciousness as being of any advantage to me in my future, although it was gradually dawning on me that I had won the hardest battle with which I had ever been confronted; and, so far as I could judge, had won it on my own terms and against considerable odds.

Indeed, in my slightly dazed phase of almost disbelief it was with some surprise that I found myself, still uniformed and anonymous-looking, ensconced in a third-class railway carriage heading southwards towards the first of my changes of train to complete the journey south. I dissolved into a kind of reverie, reflecting in some shock about my experiences of the previous weeks. The train, which was a 'slow' one, stopped at a station to pick up a few passengers, at which I took but little heed.

However, the carriage door was suddenly opened and in trooped a strangely colourful and noisy band of people – about five or six in number. One and all were attired in a kind of second-hand smartness, but enlivened by bright accessories. The two women were both carrying extraordinarily large and glittery hand bags, and both wore heavy make-up and rather cheap looking dangling earrings and bracelets: their mascara was black and their cheeks rouged and each was smoking. One was probably in her late fifties, ravaged and coarse of complexion, whilst the other, in her early twenties, still had about her something of a fast-fading beauty and pert attraction. The men, of whom there were three, were ranging in age from twenty to fifty – the eldest specially striking in a chalk-striped double-breasted suit and dotted bow-tie, whilst the two others both employed curiously mismanaged flirtations with taste, apparently feeling unwilling to allow any of their fabrics or colours to find happy sanctuary in each others' company. All of the men showed-off expensive-looking chocolate-coloured suede shoes, whilst the two ladies preferred the adventure of dizzyingly high heals of very fetching primary colours.

They seemed to enter the carriage almost simultaneously, in a rush like a driven flock of geese, flinging themselves down with admirable enthusiasm on to the bunks, laughing and exchanging flippancies with each other, their voices in no way moderated: I found it fascinating and agreeable. Such was my retirement from the world, at Queen's Park, that I failed to recognize their species until clues from their conversation filled-in their background.

They were, as was made clear, part of the theatrical company, which had just ended its Christmas Pantomime run for a short season in the little town at which our train had stopped. One could not fail to be impressed at the manner in which their on-stage performances had been encouraged, by each and all of them, to overtake them in their everyday life.

"Oh, you were wonderful, darling." "Yes, dear." "I love him, darling." "I'm starting in rep. next week, dear." "I absolutely can't bear it, dear."

It was a non-stop, it seemed, put on almost exclusively for my benefit. I was overtaken by the charm of it, and had I not been so incredibly 'temperamentally unsuited' would no doubt have been tempted to join them in their own private game of charades, a game destined, one felt, to have no winners in the foreseeable future – at least, not in the profession of their choice. But sometimes, of course, even the second rate provided an encouraging boost to those in recovering circumstances, and certainly to those addicted to the bizarre.

Alas, however, two stops on and I was forced to leave the happy band in order to join my connecting train. Their farewell to me, even though I had not actually spoken, was gushing and warm and fun. Who needed sincerity? And at least I learned the word 'soubrette.'

It was at about five o'clock that I at last made my way to what now seemed my distant home.

I suppose that disappointment should never be unexpected or be found hurtful, apart from when felt in romantic matters of the heart. Alas, however, upon actually sitting down and apprising my mother and father of my planned escape attempt from the RAF, and its successful outcome, I was utterly unprepared for the blast of hostility which came from them both, and especially from my father, whose coldness toward me was in evidence for almost twenty-five years – and was very disillusioning for me. My mother's I was able to understand as her brains operated on a different and simpler set of controls than those of my father.

From the distance of time I still find it rather hard to explain how their reactions could have arisen, and very difficult to comprehend their reason for such hostility toward me. I was young, healthy, inoffensive, and quite happy in disposition. All I wanted, *needed*, was to be left alone to observe my little section of the world and its people for a year or so, in an effort to absorb its flavours and to pick the path that *I* had chosen in order to try to carve out my personal survival on my own terms. There must have been some strong instinct, inborn, not made by me, which dictated unceasingly that I should not allow myself to become enmeshed in a situation in life from which I might never extricate myself.

Without doubt that was the period when I began to distance myself from *any* form of parental influence. For a short while I continued to reside in their house, leading a strangely withdrawn life, rather like that of an extremely reclusive old-age pensioner. Ike and his family became my only friends. I severed all connection with anyone from Queen's Park: a small number of mere nodding acquaintances remained.

Very rare encounters with some of those denizens, who enquired about my Service record, resulted in their raised eyebrows and decidedly quizzical, or even alarmed, looks aimed at me when I admitted that I had been discharged for reasons of 'nerves.'

After a very few of such encounters I ceased to furnish them with that armoury for attacking me. Rather did I resort to: 'weak chest', or some such innocuous-sounding reason.

(Later in life I was reminded of this need for caution when an old Traveller said to me: "My son, I don't never tell *no lies at all* – well, only just to get meself out've trouble, don't you know.") It was yet another lesson to learn.

There can be little doubt that my service career, if that is what it can be charitably termed, wreaked a certain havoc with my nervous system; more than I realised at the time. In fairness, I now believe that my true state of mind, when I returned, passed completely over the heads of both my mother and father – so furious were they at having their plans for my military sojourn so rudely thwarted. They were, without doubt, completely unaware of the *desperation* which I had suffered in the course of effecting my escape. Nothing that I did, or so it appeared, fitted into the role, which they had planned for me. It was, for them, as though my whole life had crashed, without the smallest glimpse of future survival within the confines they had set for themselves and, optimistically, for me too.

Even twenty years forward in time their outlook could possibly have been so different. No longer might my future have seemed, even in their eyes, so irredeemable. The time was to approach when the aim of life, work, and relationships, began to be geared towards the achieving of *happiness* as the ultimate goal. Naïve possibly, but not to be dismissed out of hand. However, we were still in 1948 and actual *happiness* was low on national priorities.

An example of the kind of meanness of spirit, which still flourished was exemplified by the attitude of our neighbour, Mrs Mercer. Her son John had returned intact from "Sig-na-pore," vacated the air-force and returned to his position in a bank. He could be spotted each morning, dark-suited, white-shirted, and ex-RAF tied, stepping nimbly from the front door and mounting a shining, new-looking, Hercules bicycle. His mother, a natural expert in all forms of hand-finished cleaning, had retained the docile machine in immaculate order throughout the entire duration of her son's stationing in "Sig-na-pore" and for the ensuing several weeks after his return to this country before receiving his discharge. The ex-airman was entitled to six week's paid leave before returning to his civilian labours. However, his mother's advice to him was not to take up the offer – or at least only for two weeks.

"Two weeks holiday is enough for *anyone,*" she asserted to my mother. However, her insensitivity and lack of charity was self-evident a few weeks later when the son of another neighbour returned from the Army, having spent four years as a Japanese prisoner of war, under, it was rumoured, exceedingly harrowing conditions. Even to the casual onlooker it was easily perceptible that the man was highly traumatised by his ordeal.

Every day over the course of the next few weeks he would leave his parents' home at about nine o'clock in the morning, neatly dressed in a navy blue, discreetly striped, double-breasted suit and polished shoes, as though he was off to work. But by some unfortunate stroke of luck, nonetheless, the inquisitive Mrs Mercer had been sharp-eyed enough to detect him wandering about on both the golf course and the common, or worse still, seated alone in a small tea shop situated amongst the little huddle of provisions stores not far from Queen's Park.

This blatant example of idleness and sloth was duly reported back to my mother, gathering malice by the yard. But a week or so later, the latent indignation and fury at such unseemly conduct in one so young reached boiling point. In his father's garage, where it had been stored throughout the war and the young man's incarceration in the Far East, was a tiny green-painted little MG sports car. The latter, after some industrious tinkering by its owner in the evenings, after his day's wanderings, was apparently coaxed back into perfect mechanical health.

And so it became the habit of the young man to drive away in it each morning, possibly for more distant and exciting destinations than the local tea shop and golf course. I found its blue-bottle-like engine, revving happily in the by-now warm spring sunshine, as it sped off up the road – its neatly dressed, slightly built, driver crouched at the wheel – a pleasure to watch. Mrs Mercer, though, appeared to be affronted by such behaviour. Impervious to the fact that he had suffered those years of almost unbearable privation at the hands of the Japanese, whilst her son John had enjoyed comparative luxury at his station near "Sig-na-pore," her irritation at the fact that he was not 'working,' as though God-driven as a matter of morality, knew no bounds.

"Huh!" she exclaimed. "It's all right for some in't it! I mean, my John's off to work every day – he can't afford to go jollifying around all day. I should think not!"

Even my mother, not a woman of excessive charity of thought, was bound to exclude herself slightly from such sentiments. But I always felt that the strong northern personality of Mrs Mercer, combined with an innate sourness of outlook, was more than even my own mother felt able to combat with much success.

It was, of course, all part of the 'know your place' boundaries of the times; such behaviour was the right of the Idle Rich only. In truth any morning spent traversing the Golden Mile of shops and café restaurants in the most expensive area of the opulent town of Bournemouth itself, would reveal scores of young men, some ex-officers on discharge-leave, others wealthy in their own right – their elegantly tailored clothes and spectacular limousines and sports cars, often tributes, one felt, to their immediate forbears' industry.

Indignation towards those in possession of 'un-earned income' as it was referred to by the then Labour Government, was not solely restricted to Queen's Park! Rumours were afoot that such 'drones' would be taxed out of existence and that, for the men at least, the full force of the New Direction of labour law would be enforced. The saloon bars soon became rife with rumours that hundreds of well-healed young gentlemen would soon find their days in a kind of Bertie Woosterish mode were to be snatched from them – only to find themselves dispatched forthwith into menial tasks such as slaughter-men or refuse-collectors! As ever, naturally, such young men were not as ill equipped to defend their idyllic life-styles as they had possibly led the ignorant to believe.

Various astute legal advisors were quick to apply their knowledge of the law and its manipulation, if lubricated with sufficient financial oil, and come up with surprising and novel-seeming alternative 'careers' which their anxious clients might consider. I was, myself, never a potential victim of that particularly objectionable-sounding law. At the time one could not but harbour a suspicion that it was the very kind of governmental power-wielding which had been so much part of the Dictatorships which our fathers had fought against so hopefully.

In any event I was heartened by the fact that, for the remainder of my lodging within the Queen's Park estate, the sight of the little MG and its discreet driver were still in evidence, which was at least a small source of comfort to me. But, at home, it was difficult to contemplate things staying as they were.

My mother virtually ceased to communicate with me – merely plonking down an occasional meal in front of me, if and when I appeared. My father was, I always suspected, more than somewhat disillusioned with his then life and became ever more unresponsive. As something of an antidote, I presume, he developed into a regular and unremitting evening drinker. His timing of his visits to the nearest public house was regular and unmissable – from eight until ten o'clock every night. To my knowledge he never became drunk, just a little flushed and even quieter than usual. There seemed little joy left in life.

The opposite fact always struck home to me whenever I was with Ike and his family. Travellers, it seemed, were forever arguing, laughing, or poking fun at one another: good spirits and enjoyment were foremost. All combined, without fail, with an optimism and enthusiasm with which all challenges were met – characteristics which have never failed to win my approval, and indeed emulation.

Despite all the foregoing, or perhaps *because* of it, I felt it time to take stock. With my 'dealing money' in my post office book, and the addition of RAF saved funds, I was in no way a victim of really straitened circumstances. In fact, for my intended needs, my provision was adequate.

(In the year 2010 it is difficult to imagine the minute sums required in order to obtain objects that today would amount to thousands of pounds – yet which, in those days, could be purchased for a fraction of such a figure.)

The time for hesitation was over. The reckless plunge must be undertaken without delay.

Chapter Eleven

A Life on Wheels

From the time that I left the air force I increased the amount of time that I spent with both Ike, his family, and a number of his still-itinerant relatives. Interestingly, and fortunately for me, Bronco and Ike were both widely known and respected amongst all the surrounding Romani families, both still on the road and those settled-down. Like all Travellers, naturally, they had their enemies too – but they were far outnumbered by those who held them in high esteem.

"Nicest fellow in the world," said a Traveller to me concerning Bronco. "Man got loads o' *loover* (money)," he declared in admiration, adding: "But he ain't a braggy man – an' if he know'd you needed it he'd soon help you out. He wouldn't see a man an' his children goo hungry, on my life." It was an example that many would aspire to, yet few could achieve.

Since the evening I had walked into their little house and told them of my 'escape' I warmed even more toward them. Their delight on hearing of my freedom put my own parents' reaction to shame. The sheer pleasure on their faces was enough for me to know an emotion rarely experienced. Even Ike's sister Annie, to whom I had hardly spoken, smiled her appreciation, whilst her newly announced fiancé Collier (so named because of his blackness) positively beamed.

"Me dear old dad always said, 'once you'm in there you'm fucked' – but you seems to have got out all right!"

Everyone laughed and old Aunt Kizzy exclaimed: "I know'd you wuz too fly to bide into that old *culli* (army), my son. You'm best off out've it, back among sensible people – not wi' a nest o' *dinilos* (fools)."

There was no arguing with that.

I had already outlined my plans with Ike and Bonny, but it was only then that I told the others of my intention to buy a waggon and horse and go off, even if alone, on the roads – Travellers' style. This information was met with a mixture of approval, shock, disbelief, and encouragement.

"If I wuz sixty year younger I'd be outa that door an' come 'long wi' you, so help me Dear Blessed God!" enthused Aunt Kizzy, coughing bronchially with the excitement of her jocularity.

"Be quiet, mother," ordered her daughter in affected disapproval. "Goo an' sit down an' bide quiet or you'll make yourself bad – an' I ain't a-gonna nuss you fru branchitees agen, I can tell you that now."

"God's cuss you – ungratefullest daughter in the world!" replied the old woman, relapsing back in her chair and lighting her clay pipe."

In the way of Travellers I did not apprise them of the actual 'depth of my pocket' as regarding my financial state, inferring rather, to their amused approval, that I was but one step above a 'dosser.' – the latter being the lowest position to which one could sink.

"Goo away!" laughed Aunt Kizzy. "I bet you'm got so much *loover* (money) as you has to keep un in two banks!"

The flippancy continued in a good-humoured way. Travellers have a sixth sense about money and can sense man's true financial state without hesitation – almost invariably correctly. Money means respect, and, as is the way with all self-employed peoples, its possession cannot help but be an indication of a man's abilities – unless, of course, he happens to be the victim of a spate of bad luck, which may strike without warning at even the most astute of operators.

I should perhaps mention that although Bronco was himself 'employed' at the time on the Municipal Tip, his attendance, and even his actual work, were largely at his own preference and completely devoid of the 'cards' and other paraphernalia which seems to hang around the necks of the majority of such workers. (In fact his independence of spirit was so taxed by the regularity of his occupation, after a lifetime of freelance toil at his own place of choice, that he abandoned the job altogether – from which time, pride restored, his natural good spirits returned.)

"I knows a man with a nice little Open Lot Dorset-shape Waggon that you could buy for the right money, kid," suggested Ike.

"Where's he to, Ike?" enquired Bonny.

"Not too far away," replied Ike cagily.

"Is it clean?" I enquired.

"Course it is," said Ike, "I wouldn't take you to see no rubbish. It ain't no cast-off from old rough Travellers – when I tells you whose got it you'll know he ain't the sort've man to harbour no buggy old things on his place."

"How much is he asking?" I enquired.

"I think he askin' fifty pounds," Ike replied. "But I 'spect you'd buy it a bit under that – with a little drink for me!" he added, smiling at the thought.

"Has he got any harness?" I asked, adding, "Or a cob, if the waggon's heavy?"

"No, it ain't heavy – a pony'd pull it easy, on my life. He give 'is word on that."

"Hm," I said, noncommittally.

"He's a dealing-man as have got it," explained Ike. "He mostly deals in motors an' he've took this waggon off a Traveller in part-exchange for a little Bedford lorry like mine."

"I bet me Uncle Siddy'd have a pony, an' some harness what he could sell you," suggested Bonny.

"Well I'll have a look at the waggon first – then fit the horse to it," I decided. "When would we go and have a look, Ike?"

"I'll ring the man up tonight at the *kitchemer* (pub) 'cos he takes all his calls there."

"Traveller?" I asked, rather unnecessarily, for who else would employ such complexities of business communication?

"Well, he is an' he ain't," admitted Ike. "His mother was one of the Bulls an' his father was a 'wide-o' *gaujo* man – anyway he's a sensible old follow an' you can have a deal with him, don't you worry."

"Well, I'll leave it with you," I said. "I'm free any time at all so whenever it suits you or him its all right with me."

It seemed that just at that time I never failed to call in to see the family on almost every day. There was thus no delay before an arrangement was made for Ike, Bonny, and me, to journey over to a small village not far from Southampton, on the edge of the New Forest, where, in a smallholding of restricted area, resided the dealing-man and his aged father – Shady and Old Shady.

Luckily Ike had explored the entire area since becoming motorised, his devoted searches for scrap-iron causing him to make lengthy journeys over a vast area around the countryside. Hence, although he had never actually visited the smallholding he was aware of the approximate piece of country in which it would be found. Eventually, we found ourselves in an area called North Baddesley, a place which appeared to be the locality of choice for a large number of settle-down Travellers – their distinctive little homes being at once recognisable to other Travellers.

As we passed by one such home, very small yet neat and well looked-after, we noticed a Romani woman cleaning the windows. Unmistakeably a Traveller both in dress and cadaverous features, she turned to face us, her lined and slightly haggard face becoming transformed with a bright smile when she realised we were Travellers.

"'Scuse me, Aunt," said Bonny politely from the lorry, "but we're lookin' to find the place of Old Shady an' his son – we hopes to do a bit of trade with 'em. Could you direct us?"

"Well, certainly I can, young man," replied the woman, her accent a strong Hampshire dialect, differing considerably from the Dorset tones of Bonny and Ike.

"You ain't far away," she continued. "You goes on down this road till you meets a cross roads, an' you turns left-handed, go through a biti water-splash an' take the fork right-handed. Then you goes on till you gets to a bit of a rough lane on your left – an' they're down on through. You can't miss 'em. Where's you *atched* (stopping) to young man?"

"We'm out agen Bournemouth, Aunt. In a bit of a *kair* (house) not so far out've Bournemouth town. Me dad's called Bronco, everyone knows *him*!"

No recognition showed in the woman's face, but she seemed pleased that Bonny had furnished her with the information. Travellers always like to know with whom they are talking.

We set off in good spirits that our information had been so easily obtained.

Ike had already met the father and son, at a horse-fair at the top end of Hampshire the previous autumn but had never before visited their place.

Soon, following our directions as best our memories served us, and luckily being united in the path we took, we soon found ourselves turning in down the lane to our destination. A crooked hand-painted sign hung unsteadily from a post, inscribed cryptically: ALL GOOD MOTORS. It was a pleasing little bungalow of asbestos and corrugated iron which confronted us, painted in green and cream with imitation beams picked-out in matt black paint at intervals along its walls. Attached on its right-hand side was a wooden lean-to with a closed door on which was written OFFICE.

Fifty feet to the left hand side stood a group of wooden buildings, one large open shed and several others, their contents being hidden behind locked garage-doors. Within the open building were a collection of commercial vehicles, mostly the 30cwt lorries and closed vans, which would appeal to Travellers. Whilst, just under cover in the forefront to one side, stood a brightly-painted Romani waggon of the square-bowed 'Dorset-shaped' Open-lot type, complete with iron-bonded wheels, shafts (so often missing), and agreeably curved steps of the 'swan-necked' design – a comparative rarity even in those days. The canvas sheet forming the roof-cover was bright and new looking, whilst the interior was traditionally set-out, with the presence of the much-revered 'Queenie' Stove. The latter, ornately fashioned in Victorian style, was of the greatest comfort to the waggon-dweller. So catholic was its taste in fuel that it was rumoured to 'burn anything from old shoes to dead cats,' (though I personally was never reduced to such straits). But without doubt they were efficient in heating a waggon, and also, having an opening top, it was a stove on which to cook one's meals, proving them to be an invaluable possession, especially during spells of inclement weather.

Old Shady, a broad-brimmed trilby hat pulled-down over his eyes, his face unshaven, was wearing an unattractive and well-seasoned striped serge suit, in a curious shade of dark grey, sump-oil and dirt. Turned-down Wellington boots completed his debonair persona. A moment later Young Shady appeared from one of the lock-ups, also wearing a trilby hat. His features were smaller and neater than those of his father and he carried the curiously subtle 'Traveller-look' which frequently haunts those of mixed parentage. His manner was eager and pleasingly informal.

"I've seen you before, kid," he remarked at once to Ike, who agreed.

"Up the horse-sales last September," he confirmed, with a slight smile.

"Well, what can I do for you, my young men?" asked Young Shady, handing his father a Woodbine cigarette, upon which he quickly inhaled, his cheeks sinking inwards alarmingly.

"Well," began Ike, "my friend here might be interested in that waggon, if you'm not askin' too much."

"Are you the buyer, or is he?" demanded Young Shady, which I could see was a perfectly reasonable question.

"He is," said Ike, adding sheepishly: "I'm only the fuckin' chauffeur!"

"We don't want to mess about all day over this, do we?" began Young Shady, pulling-down his hat brim in an echo of his father, "so I'll ask you a silly price. I only took it in against a lorry 'cos I know the man, an' I often have a bit of trade with him. But waggons ain't a lot of good to me – I'm a motor-man nowadays. It's a different generation, ain't that right? So I tell you what I'll ask you one price and one only and that's fifty pounds – and that's giving it to you, you know that."

"Can I have a proper look?" I requested, for by that time, having studied many waggons belonging to Ike's relatives, and others also, I had some idea of what to investigate.

"Course you can – you won't find no faults there!" declared Young Shady with the self-confidence and assurance which was the hallmark of his trading personality: for better or worse it is not much in evidence outside the private world of old-fashioned traders today.

"You can go and ask anyone you like to 'spect him," he rashly asserted, "an' if there's one bit of rot in the trolley or the wheels then I'll *give* un to you. I can't be nor fairer than that, can I *mush* (man)?"

Old Shady gazed wordlessly at us, enjoying the scene. For a moment or so all was quiet, punctuated only by the heavy rasping coughs he emitted after every inhalation on his Woodbine.

"Them fags is killin' me," he remarked.

"An' if they don't then me mam will – she keeps tellin' you to give 'em up, but you takes no fuckin' notice of her –proper old *dinilo* (fool)."

Ike, Bonny, and I smiled faintly, though knowing that it was unlikely, after a lifetime's addiction, that the old man would oblige her request.

"Well, boys," he observed, hoping to change the subject from his smoking, "make my son a bid. No good standin' about like this – that ain't gonna buy the baby a new frock, is it?"

I had examined the little waggon to the best of my knowledge, and felt it was undoubtedly worth an offer. By that time in my life amongst Travellers I had learnt that nobody ever pays what is asked for it, whatever the object. Hence I decided to offer forty-five pounds and await the result.

"I tell you what I'll do," I began. "I'll give you forty-five pounds for the waggon – that'll help a lame dog over a stile!"

Young Shady stared silently at me for a moment before adopting a slightly hurt expression.

"I couldn't take it, kid, and the fact is I've asked you too little – you knows that. Ain't that right, Dad?"

"You're right, my son," affirmed his father. "But it's your business since I retired an' I ain't goin' to interfere." He relapsed into another fit of coughing, to continue croakily, "but I know this, young man, if I wanted a waggon I knows I'd never find a sounder one nor a lighter one for that kind of money, strike me dead if I could!"

Ike had signalled privately to me that he considered the waggon well worth the money, and I myself liked it too. The bargaining was merely a matter of pride.

"I'll give you forty-five pounds," I repeated stolidly. "I've got the money here."

"I know that, kid," said Young Shady. "I ain't worried about that – I knows who I can trust and who I can't. If you never had the money on you, and we shook hands on the deal, you could take the waggon an' pay me when you like: I knows I'd get me money, I ain't worried about that."

This, of course, was the flattering encouragement – especially as he knew full well that it was not an offer, which I would take up. It was a tempter.

The haggling went on and on, even seeing us through several cups of tea. The latter was brought out for us in large coloured mugs by the mother of Young Shady, who rejoiced in the name of Pemberline Bull. She was an unmistakeably Romani woman in both features and dress. Her expression was rather forbidding and her plenteous gold jewellery and large hoop earrings all sat easily against her gnarled brown skin. As is not in my experience uncommon with the children of mixed parentage, known as *posh rats* (half-blood, literally), Old Shady and his wife had only one child. As it happened Young Shady had inherited the Romani ability to survive in the world of the self-employed, yet was without the Romani urge to wander. Eventually, I could see that something must be done or the deal would fall apart.

"I tell you what I will do – and it's my last bid, on my life I won't make another."

The atmosphere tensed, and staring unblinkingly at him I stated my final offer: "I'll give you forty-eight pounds and not one penny more – hold out your hand!"

Sensing it was all or nothing, Young Shady slapped palms with me – and all was concluded: I owned my first Romani waggon.

Little did I know then what the journey ahead entailed, nor dream of the numbers of waggons and horses that were to pass through my hands as time and tide proceeded before me. In the manner of such transactions I paid Young Shady the cash there and then, upon receipt of which he returned a pound to me as 'luck money'.

"Well boys," he said, "you take the waggon when you like, though I hope it won't be too long as I could do with the space. Anyway I'll leave it to you."

"Me cousin Righteous has got one o' them low-loaders as I can lend," said Ike. "We'll try to get over Saturday afternoon or Sunday at the latest."

With which we said our farewells and drove off towards home.

I should perhaps mention here that it was considered an unusual step for anyone like myself to assume the mantle of a horse-drawn Traveller's life-style – almost unknown in fact. And, of course, long before the appearance of the considerable numbers of so-called New Age Travellers, whose ramshackle conglomerations were to meander about the countryside from the nineteen sixties on through the 'seventies and 'eighties, gradually diminishing in quantity, whilst many transferred to the accommodation of old buses or converted horse-boxes. Their lives and those of Romanies rarely collided, and their congress was made even more unlikely when each group discovered that their aims and ambitions were diametrically opposed in almost every way. The innate dynamism and ambition of the Romanies did not fall in with the laid-back sloth of the dazed-seeming Hippy 'New Agers'. Hence the two groups maintained entirely separate lives, rarely, if ever, travelling or stopping together.

After some discussion Ike and I decided that the best place for me to take the waggon, until I had bought horse and harness and was ready for the road, was to the property of a settled-down Traveller near to Ringwood in Hampshire. Originally from Devon the man, called 'Tippy-tongue Joe' had been fortunate to buy some ten acres of land and obtain permission for a bungalow to be built on it, in which he lived. The land was a mixture of field and scrubland and he regularly allowed Travellers to pull-in there for a few weeks providing he knew who they were. Ike and his father Bronco knew him well and had no hesitation in contacting him by telephone to inquire as to his readiness to accommodate the waggon until I was ready and fully equipped for 'the off.' Fortunately, he proved more than willing to agree to the request, so all was arranged to our mutual satisfaction.

One of the first things that struck me when I had removed myself from the cloying environment of Queen's Park and embraced the Travellers' world more fully, was my astonishment at the size and variety of its population. Its facets were multifarious in class, habitation, and condition. Whilst, besides the undeniably 'Gypsy' people, at once recognisable to the casual observer, there were the innumerable hoards of those whose Romani blood was so diluted, like that of some Jewish people I believe, that they fell, a little unhappily, into a half-world – frequently seeming to move from one social encounter to another with no great sureness of where they *really* belonged. In those days, from my own experience, large numbers of horse-dealers, 'general' dealers, and even lesser smallholders, were obviously enlivened in their personalities, and their achievements, by their part-Romani ancestry. (A claim I might sometimes adopt for myself if I have pulled-off a minor business success!)

The strength of such family genes is to be wondered at in awe. I can call to mind at once a family who I have known for fifty years or more as an example. The mother figure had a Romani mother and a *gaujo* father. She herself married a completely *gaujo* man from farming stock.

They lived in a smallholding in Devon and produced four sons and a daughter. Although they went to school in the normal way, not one of the children followed the *gaujo* path. They sought no regular employment nor took any of the normal routes. Instead, the boys began dealing in horses from a young age, prospering to some degree, before later becoming motor-dealers of great astuteness. All the boys married Romani girls, and the daughter later married a Romani man. Their children are following in their footsteps and a renewal of the Traveller-dynasty has been created. It is a refreshing turn of events.

(I recently heard on the television a member of a well-respected Romani family – in the year 2010 – saying, "…..Travellers are the most self-sufficient people there are. They are all self-employed, and can get their livings anywhere in the world……" It did my heart good to hear him say this. What a tonic after the constant presentation of Travellers as 'victims' in society by social workers and the like whose main ambition, it often appears, is to prise Travellers from their traditional life and press them into council housing and lowly nine-to-five jobs – *just like everyone else*. No encouragement for Travellers to make a stand in defending their traditional ways of life, of course!)

On the Saturday at about noon I was seated in the back room drinking tea with Rosina, Aunt Kizzy, and Ike when the peace of the little street was disturbed by the roars of a mighty lorry engine and the harsh rumblings of a deep klaxon horn.

"Cah! Hark at that," exclaimed Ike. "That'll be Righteous – the noisy cunt!"

He had no intention of being malicious, and we all smiled contentedly. A few moments later and a man, who I presumed to be Cousin Righteous, entered. He was in his mid-twenties with a mass of black curls hanging over his strangely Mexican-looking features. His rather dramatic appearance, thick set and stocky, was further enhanced by his black suit and startlingly white shirt.

"You'm smart, Cuz.," observed Ike. "I likes your suit – new ain't it?"

"Yeah, I'm just breakin' it in," smiled Righteous, disclosing two gold front teeth.

"I likes to see a man dressed in a nice suit of clothes," grinned Aunt Kizzy approvingly.

"How's you Aunt Kizzy, an' you Aunt Rose?" he enquired solicitously.

"Better for seein' you, young man," remarked Aunt Kizzy roguishly.

"Bide quiet, mother," reproved Rosina. "You'm wusser'n an old *lubni* (whore)."

Righteous laughed and offered some Black Beauty and a cigarette paper to the women, which they accepted graciously. I had not started smoking yet.

"I'd a-sooner go wi'out me bread an' meat than a bit o' baccy," mused Aunt Kizzy, her twisted fingers soon devoting themselves to the manufacture of an elegant roll-up.

Bonny arrived just then and he, Ike, and Righteous applied themselves to their cigarettes prior to leaving in the elongated low-loader on the journey to collect my waggon.

Outside I noticed that the lorry was of some age, though well painted and clean. The legend 'The Dorset Queen' was inscribed along the top of the windscreen, and a pile of loose chains and hooks and other accoutrements of the transporting business were roped-down just behind the cab.

"I don't even know where we're fuckin' goin,' Ike," laughed Righteous with the optimistic indifference of a Traveller.

"Down to Lands End," said Bonny, his face solemn.

"Like its grandmother's cunt, we are," replied Righteous, sure of his ground.

After it was explained to him the exact destination that we were aiming for he rather took the wind from our sails by crying out:

"What! Fuckin' hell, *mush* (man), I knows that place like me farver's! I must a-bin there fifty times. Poxy little lane it is to get round an' all. You has to back an' forward 'bout twenty times to get a long motor down there."

The lorry cab was wide enough to accommodate the four of us side by side without undue squash and we set off in good spirits. Righteous was a proficient, if rather fast, driver and we made good time. As he forecast, from past visits, his attempts to negotiate the lorry into the rough track were of some hazard owing to its size, the ever present risk of scraping the body sides against the gatepost occasioning slight agitation in the mind of the driver. However, his natural good spirits combined with a certain skill, achieved success with the least amount of tension that one might have expected.

As we turned down towards the barn we saw that the waggon had been pulled out for ease of loading.

At our arrival an ancient greyhound appeared, barking without much spirit, followed by Old Shady, the eternal Woodbine hanging from his mouth.

"I knowed 'twas yous," he observed, triumphant at his flash of perspicacity. He added, "My Shady's down the Auction – he'll be back directly if you needs him."

"Nah! That's all right, Uncle," Righteous assured him amiably. "We'll soon have her up on the back an' get on, 'cos we got a fair few miles to go, an' I wants to get back 'fore it gets too dimsy dark if we can."

On familiar ground Righteous immediately affixed a chain to the lock of the waggon, removing the shafts first, and attaching it to the winch began to haul it gently up the runners and on, forwards, until it was just behind the cab. With the assistance of Ike, who then fancied himself an expert in all things mechanical, they had soon secured the little waggon firmly, with the shafts tied on underneath and the steps stored inside.

I looked on hesitantly.

"She won't shift, kid," said Righteous. "Ain't no way she can come off there, like me dead farver."

The way out of the lane was negotiated more smoothly than coming in, and we were soon off, spinning along to the main road, which would take us to Ringwood, and thence to the land of Tippy-tongue Joe.

This was a property that both Ike and Bonny knew well as they conducted quite regular dealings with Joe, so there would be no difficulty in locating the correct property.

As it happened it was no more than early afternoon when we arrived at the entrance gates, over which was suspended a lengthy rustic sign announcing, rather surprisingly: THE DOUBLE J PIGGERIES.

The gates were unlocked and we headed over some scrubby pasture land, on a narrow track, towards the only visible dwelling, an astonishingly smart bungalow of a rather continental design. A white Alsatian emerged from a large kennel set a little to the left of the bungalow, barking and growling with psychotic fury from the end of a twelve or fifteen feet chain, attached to an iron stake. The chain provided an arc from which the dog was prevented further access in its attempts to maul unknown visitors. A faded notice leaned against the wall with the cryptic warning: AWARE DOG.

At the sound of our motor, coupled with the deafening barks, growls, and howls of frustration from the demented animal in its efforts to repel us, the front door was opened by an extremely fat and unhealthy-looking man of middle years, his hair white, and his face the colour of pickled-cabbage. He was wearing a blue suit, silk tie, and tan jodhpur boots. His chubby fingers were complimented by the presence of several heavy gold rings set with diamonds. It was no mean demand on one's credibility to assimilate the fact that this was a Romani man. His disguise was impressive: only his tan jodhpur boots were his private symbol of a Travellery look.

On recognising three of his visitors his pale lined face dissolved into something akin to a smile. Carrying the formality of his attire to its conclusion he held out a hand to Ike and shook his warmly.

Surprisingly when he spoke his nickname became obvious, fascinatingly combined with a heavy South Devon accent, the latter as strong as though he had strode the streets of Newton Abbot only the day before.

"How be you than my booty?" he enquired, continuing, poetically, though stutteringly: "Yere, 'tis nice to see'ee. You'm so welcome as the flowers in May!"

It is difficult to convey the actuality of his 'tippy-tongue' but it would seem to consist of a vocal displacement of either tonsular or trachean complications, causing a sort of bifurcated, gulping, stammer to interrupt most vocal attempts. In his case, I learnt, it was of a genetic inheritance. His great uncle Crimea having been the first recorded member to be known as 'Tippy-tongue.' However, it had never markedly lowered the ability of those in its grip to wrestle supremely well with all life's problems of survival. Almost all his relatives existed in states of splendour, which could only be envied, if not admired.

"My, you've growed-up a bit since I last seen 'ee," he said to Bonny, to his slight embarrassment.

"I sees you've fetched the waggon over, then – is this the young feller it 'longs to?" he enquired, gulping and 'tippy-tonguing' as one would have expected from his nickname.

"That's right, Uncle Joe," agreed Ike respectfully. "He's going on the roads wi' un soon enough – fax the matter is as soon as he can find hisself a *grai* (horse). We calls him the Romany Rai!"

At this Joe became convulsed with laughter and pleasure and at once launched into a somewhat vibrating version of the old melody *The Romani Rai*. Striking a flamboyant pose he burst out into song:

> *"Dwellers in cities work for a wage,*
> *Gold could not buy for me such a cage.*
> *Out on the common beneath the blue sky,*
> *Who is as free as the Romani Rai?*
> *Masters I smile at, none calls me a slave,*
> *Strolling in the heather, monarch am I –*
> *Who is a king like the Romani Rai ....*

(here he threw out his arms in greater animation for the chorus)

> *"I'm a Romani Rai, I'm a true diddikai,*
> *I build my mansions beneath the blue sky,*
> *I lives in a tent, and I don' pay no rent –*
> *That's why they calls me the Romani Rai."*

The performance left us all somewhat awestruck; respect, nostalgia and sentiment struck us forcibly. It was, as ever with Travellers, the delight in experiencing the unexpected, in what would appear to be completely unlikely circumstances that was so rewarding. It was a pleasure to see a man, who for most of his business life had found it necessary to endeavour to hide his origins, being able to let himself go completely and relax in the comfort of his own people in circumstances demanding no subterfuge nor deceit. It was an added pleasure for me to see that, convinced of my friendship, as opposed to mere acquaintanceship, with Ike and Bonny he had been relaxed enough to show me a glimpse of his true self – no matter how transient such a disclosure might be.

After a few polite enquiries about relatives and their health, he went inside for a camel overcoat and then showed us the place which he thought to be most suitable as temporary housing for the waggon.

After this was completed he invited us into the kitchen for a cup of tea before our departure. It was luxurious beyond our dreams, and had but recently been fitted with a new floor of Italian marble tiles which sparkled cheerily up at us. (My mother, I knew at once, would have been impressed to a point of light-headedness at the expensive quality of the fittings, both kitchenware and furnishings.)

Joe's wife was as small as he was large. Her smart apparel would not have been out of place in any upper middle-class villa. Only when she spoke would her Travellery origins be revealed. She too was a native of Devonshire, and of indubitably cheerful disposition. Bottle-blonde and lively she possessed an admirable freedom of expression which I had found to be lacking in any of the ladies of Queen's Park whom I had encountered. At only one point did she seem slightly out of temper and that was when their son's fiancé telephoned to speak to him. But he was absent, they knew not where, and both were a trifle put out that he had not apprised them of either his whereabouts nor of his planned hour of return. (Travellers always like to keep in constant touch with their children. Not, of course, so easy before the universally adopted Mobile Phone.)

"That was Anne-Marie," she told Joe. "An' Joe-boy told her he was gonna be home all day – an' what could I tell the gal? I ain't gonna tell no lies for him – he can go an' fuck his grandmother!"

These matronly sentiments reduced us all to laughter. The barriers were down!

She took a gold lighter from her capacious handbag, then a packet of filter-tip cigarettes, and lit one. Joe reached over and also withdrew one for himself – offering one to each of us.

"No thanks, Uncle Joe – I'm tryin' to give 'em up," smiled Bonny.

But Ike accepted gratefully. A rather soft-scented tobacco smoke wafted around the room in the kind of clouds which would, today, strike fear into the hearts of all but the most dedicated of inhalers.

Finishing our tea we left the bungalow by the back door, thus avoiding the savage dog straining at his chain in uncontrolled fury, just visible to us.

"I hope that chain holds," said Ike. "That fuckin' *juke* (dog) would *muller* (kill) you if he got loose."

It took us little time to off-load the waggon and push it around to the location that Joe had suggested.

Tippy-tongue gave it his seal of approval.

"If I wuz fifty years younger I'd be off in it meself," he declared. "Finest life in the world – specially on a nice spring day. That's a handsome little waggon, my boy, an' nice and light – a pony could pull un."

No limit was put on the time that I could store the waggon there, but I was more than anxious to begin my new life as soon as possible during the spring. My search for a horse and harness was all that remained for me.

Anticipation, trepidation, excitement, even fear, were the emotions that assailed me as the days passed. The disgust of my parents knew no bounds when told of my advanced plans. My complete dismissal of their core-values of respectability, conforming without question, and complete integration into the 'blue-collar' or even 'white-collar' form of existence was something of a severe body blow to them. Though just *why* their hostility was so intense remained a mystery to me.

Looking back, of course, my own little rebellion against a prescribed format was a little ahead of its time. Had it occurred during the later, more eccentric and freer, years of the nineteen sixties it would have created much less animosity.

In any event, with the strangeness of chance and coincidence, which dogs us all, my quest for equine possessions were unexpectedly fulfilled. Some little distance from Bronco's home, in one of the myriad lanes and streets of the neighbourhood there resided an ageing General Dealer (Rag and bone man) named Ernie Wicker. Having attained the age of seventy he had decided to retire and intended to sell his horse, trolley, and harness. Having heard of this Bronco sent Ike to look at the items, and instructed him to tell me the result – which he did. Thus we arranged for me to inspect the horse and harness the next day. Enquiries from me elicited the information that the pony was 'a hard-toothed Bay mare, about 14 hands, nice and 'cobby,' and that the harness was "a good white-metal set, with plenty of wear into it."

We found the establishment of Ernie Wicker with no trouble. It was a small gated yard, nearly filled with scrap-iron of a domestic variety, and bales of mixed rags under tarpaulins – all the results of his daily rounds out 'calling' in the area.

Ernie Wicker himself was a striking figure, of a kind long since disappeared. Wearing a faded velour hat over home-cut white hair, his face was long and hawk-like. Around his neck was knotted a red and white spotted scarf, whilst over a Derby tweed waistcoat he wore a brown overcoat, or 'smock' as they were then known. Corduroy trousers and heavy brown boots completed his wardrobe. He was, undeniably, an 'old-fashioned' man.

We found him sitting in an old armchair in a corner of the yard, smoking a pipe from which brackish-coloured smoke exuded in sporadic clouds. A small brindle whippet bitch lay placidly at his feet.

"Hello, Mr Wicker," Ike greeted him politely. "We heared you was sellin' up. Only I might try to buy the iron and rags offen you, an' me friend might try to buy the old pony and harnesh."

Mr Wicker squinted at us through the pipe-smoke, a non-committal half-smile crossing his face.

"Ah – I wondered what you was after, young men – You'll be Bronco's oldest boy, i'n't that right?" he remarked to Ike.

"That's right, Mr Wicker," replied Ike, with an air of affected respect that he always assumed when dealing with non-Travellers. Though in this particular case he had a certain liking for Ernie Wicker who was known locally as a 'fly old customer' by all and sundry. The Travellers always hinted their belief that there was more than a hint of gypsy in his pedigree. There had been a Mrs Wicker, but she had recently passed away which was partly the cause of his retirement: they had no offspring to follow on in their footsteps.

"How is your father?" asked the old dealer, solicitously.

"Lovely, thank you, Mr Wicker," said Ike.

"Well, I've got bad news an' I got good news for you, boys," he continued. "First thing to say is as I've sold all me iron an' rags to Alfie Orchard – no more'n two hours ago: he's pickin' 'em up directly, first thing in the morning. " He hesitated for this news to sink in.

"Now about the *grai* (horse)," he said, grinning at Ike after using *Romani* talk: "Well, she'm still up for sale, an' the harness, an' the trolley – all sound, the lot of 'em."

"We ain't got no use for the trolley," replied Ike, "but me Uncle Siddy 'd buy it if you axed him the right money – I could 'phone him up at the public tonight if you like."

"All right, thanks Ike. There'll be a drink in it for you if we has a deal. Now, how about the mare and harness?"

I did not need to examine her closely as I had seen her in the streets on most days, pulling the trolley during Ernie's scrap collecting forays around the houses. I knew she was docile, quiet and traffic-proof. Her only disadvantage was that she had not recently lived outdoors at night, nor, to the best of my knowledge had she ever been tethered by a 'plug-chain' as was the necessity for Travellers' horses on unfenced land and roadside verges. However, it was spring and the nights were getting warmer. The tethering could be accomplished after a little time of trial. We explained the situation, and the locality of where my waggon was stored.

Being very parochial the paths of Mr Wicker and Tippy-tongue Joe had not crossed, though an expression which passed over his face at the mention of Joe's name made me suspect that he at least *knew* of him. Of course, in actuality, their worlds did not have much reason to cross. The legendary earnings of Joe were said to be assessed in 'telephone numbers' (so large were their totals) whilst the more old-fashioned Ernie's were more of the 'peanuts' amounts.

The latter's boast was that he worked on the principle that 'Little Apples Taste Sweet.' That principle is one which I have adopted throughout most of my life and I am convinced that its resultant stress levels, as opposed to strain imposed by higher-pressure pursuits, can only improve one's chances of achieving a longer existence, played out in reasonable health.

"She's a good quiet mare, so quiet as a child could drive her – never spooked by nothing, not bombs, nor tanks nor steam-rollers. I've had her for three years, s'know, and I can say, without one word of a lie, as she's one of the best as I ever owned – and that's sayin' something, believe me."

"Will you put a price on her, and the harness as well?" I asked, impatient as ever.

"I won't insult you and ask if you'm a serious buyer, 'cos I kin see with me two eyes as you are. Anyway I'll ask you a sensible price, not one to make you go white-faced. I'll take ninety pounds for the lot!"

It was more than I had hoped. It was more than a Traveller would have asked at that time for a cob, but it had the advantage of my knowing the animal to be sound and tractable, hopefully without any of the 'dodges,' which frequently beset the animals which had been in the hands of Travellers.

"*Kekker* (no). Bid un!" breathed Ike to me softly.

"Oh dear, I couldn't do that," I replied mournfully to the asking price.

"Well, that's it, she've only been on sale for two days. Fact is that that feller Bobby Lonsdale wants to buy her, Noah's Tom told me so this morning."

"Bobby Lonsdale!" repeated Ike in some disgust. "He won't give you nothin'! All he buys ends up down the meat factory for dog food."

"That's as may be – you can't take no notice of all you hear," replied the old man coldly.

"My friend's only young an' he ain't got all the money in the world, so try an' have a deal wi' un, Mr Wicker, goo on!"

"Huh! I ain't got all the fuckin' money in the world – not even a half of it – don't talk to me about no money." He affected to be quite aggrieved. But he was a dealing-man of enough calibre not to reveal his true reactions.

"Ninety pounds!" I exclaimed. "How do you work that out?"

"Seventy pounds for the mare, an' twenty for the harness."

"I'll give you seventy pounds for the lot," I offered, staring hard at him.

"I couldn't do it," he came back apologetically. "I know they say that one bidder's worth twenty lookers on but that's too low ..... There's only one thing I can say – as your tryin' an' I like a trier – that is, you gimme eighty-five pounds an' not a penny less, an' you've got yourself a deal. That's fair, ain't it, s'know?"

Caught up in the excitement of the deal, even though it was one of my first on such a scale, I knew that we would eventually meet.

Hence, after several more to and fro bids and rejections of them we finally shook hands at the total sum of eighty pounds plus another pound for a thirty-feet long 'plus-chain' which Ike discovered behind the stable, a little rusty but sound, fitted with a swivel at each end – an essential appendage to any such tethering device in order to avoid its twisting and kinking through its length.

I left twenty pounds to seal the deal with Ernie Wicker, agreeing to collect the mare and harness within the next three to four days.

There was a certain amount of organisation to perform. I eventually decided that the best course of action was to take the horse, harness, and my personal belongings and clothes over to Tippy-tongue Joe's property and start out from there. Once more, a distant relative of Ike, with a horse box trailer, was brought in for assistance. Within the Traveller fraternity there is no shortage of contacts in whatever form they are required: speedily, without delay, their services can be relied upon, immediate cash settlements being their only absolute law.

My removal from Queen's Park was curiously smooth once the hour of departure had arrived. My parents, in a fit of unexpected extravagance, had obtained a telephone, and so any need that I might have to contact them was eased.

In those days of few motor vehicles, with no mobile 'phones, and no great number of land-lines either, communication was hazardous and difficult, whilst actual distances seemed greater than they were.

I had arranged to spend one night in my waggon at Tippy-tongue Joe's before setting off the next day under horse-drawn power in the vague direction of Berkshire or Surrey – all totally unknown country to me. My possessions were few: one suit, a few shirts, ties, and several silk scarves. For daily wear I chose a black velour hat, silk scarf and shirt and plain waistcoat, 'fall-front' corduroy trousers (made Travellers'-style by a little shop in Wareham for only ten shillings), tan-coloured jodhpur boots, and a pleated-back twill jacket which I had purloined from the fastnesses of a Country Show near Salisbury the previous year. Coupled with two or three mugs, plates, and knives and forks, my only other necessities for the outdoor life were an iron kettle, a black stew pot, and a hoop-handled frying pan. And lastly a kettle-iron or 'crane', which a blacksmith of old Mr Wickers' acquaintance had soon made up for me. At five shillings it seemed expensive but probably was not.

After numerous visits to Waggon-Travellers, in the surrounding countryside, I had picked-up the rudiments of lighting stick-fires, from observation, and even the art of preparing rough-hewn meals – the fat-content of which would have been sternly disapproved of by today's dieticians.

The Yog – and Kettle Cranes

"You cain't beat the taste o' victuals what's cooked outside on the *yog* (fire)," was an opinion that I heard voiced incessantly by its practitioners over the years. It is not an opinion that I have case to challenge.

The iron cooking-pots, though by then mostly enamel-lined, hoop-handled and usually with tin lids, were obtainable in the more rural country-town hardware stores, as were the hoop-handled frying pans. Both of the last two items were still used by older-style countrywomen on their open-fire cooking ranges, as indeed were the large round black iron kettles too. The latter was of great pleasure to me; its charmingly rounded shape and tall, arched, fixed handle provided an extraordinarily appealing sight as it hung, singing, in the flames, from the 'crane.'

Although I was starting my journey alone it was not my ambition to subside into the condition of a lone eccentric for too long, at the very least I hoped to find Travellers *en route* with whom I might spend some time.   My other ambition was to furnish myself with a dog, as companion and guard.   For the latter purpose my encounter with the ferocious animal belonging to Tippy-tongue Joe had decided me that an Alsatian was the right breed for me to seek out, though not a white one. For some unknown reason I have never been anything but repelled by white livestock, either animal or fowl: it is one of my quirks of opinion, and not one that I can understand.

I will not bore the reader with the details of my actions and movements up until I departed from Joe's property. Suffice to say that all went without a hitch, the transportation of the mare being achieved without mishap.

She was a dark, dappled bay with four white socks, and her spring coat was glistening in the sun on the day we left.

On the day prior to my departure I had decided to burn all my correspondence, forms, ration book, air-force documents, and indeed any form of identification which might have lain about my person. I changed my name to one about which I felt there was a faintly raffish air, but which I abandoned after a short duration! In those far-off carefree days it was all that was necessary to emerge as from a chrysalis into one's new persona.   Later, when travelling with a horse and waggon, I was frequently stopped by police, on bicycles or in 'control' cars, and asked for my, "name and age?" Despite my change in both I was never re-questioned nor ever asked for *proof* of identity – which, in retrospect, seems rather exhilarating.

Food rationing was, in theory, still enforced. But I found that most village shops would unhesitatingly serve me with bacon or butter, or tea or sugar, with no more than a wink when I explained that I had lost my ration book. I believe that many of them found it hard to accept that, years after the war had finished, we were one of the last countries in Europe to be so bowed down by austerity, even though we were the victors!

By a very odd trick of memory-failure I find it impossible fully to call to mind the first journey that I ever undertook, from Joe's bungalow to a piece of wasteland near to Southampton. I recollect that my attempts to remain on minor back roads were not always successful and that the area into which I was moving seemed to be becoming more and more crowded: it was as though I was a stranger on another planet. A great loneliness swept over me.

And then, passing through the outskirts of a little town called Netley Marsh, I came upon a rough and litter-strewn green, upon which, to my surprise and delight, there sat three waggons, all rather ramshackle and square-bowed in shape. Their horses, six or seven in number, were pegged some distance apart across the width of the green.

Two fires were burning, around which several adults were crouched, eating, whilst a gaggle of small children were playing nearby with broken prams and tyre-less bicycles. A few rather dispirited mongrel dogs emerged from beneath the waggons but were shouted back with the customary cries of: "Goo an' lay-down dogs!"

I pulled-up the mare and jumped down from the waggon footboard, on which I had been riding, perched in readiness for a sudden descent, if needs be.

As I gazed toward the waggons I smiled inwardly at the thought that, unknown to the Travellers round their fires, this had been my first journey into my shadowy future with a horse and waggon. Wiser was it, I decided, to try to give the impression that I was a hardened veteran of such a life.

Upon sighting us, each and every horse took up the customary position, which is unfailingly adopted when they are confronted by the unexpected appearance of strangers with a waggon. They stood stock-still and stared. The people, too, sat unmoved by their fires, also staring with curiosity in an attempt to identify me.

Thus it was with some relief and pleasure that I recognised one of the older men as being a member of Old Siddy's family of brothers and sisters: only about sixty years old he was one of the youngest brothers – with over a score in his family at hand to ease each others' pangs of loneliness should they arise. I had previously encountered him at a

Wimborne horse-sale the previous autumn, when Old Siddy and no fewer than ten of his brothers and sisters were also present.

He rose to his feet as I drew nearer and I saw that his kinship to Old Siddy was undeniable. He was just a younger version in every way: even his slightly squinting eyes were showing signs of the steady watering which had long beset those of his older brother, and, I was later to observe, those of a number of his sisters too. Luckily, he resembled Old Siddy in character too, which was to his advantage in all ways. They were both possessed of considerable charm, in their own way, and had the gift of *natural* good manners.

"I knows you, young man," he said, advancing towards me and shaking hands. "I seen you with me cousin Bronco's boy, an; me oldest brother Siddy down the Wimborne 'block' (horse sale) last year – do you mind the time?"

I assured him that I did, and that I remembered it as being a very good day.

"Which way's you headed, iffen you don't mind me axin'?" he asked, by which time a younger man and a youth had sauntered up to us.

"Nice little turnout – would you have a chop waggons, *mush*?" enquired the younger man, who proved to be the son-in-law of Old Siddy's brother who was named Liberty I learned.

"No, I don't want to part from it – but thank you all the same," I replied, making sure there was no hesitation in my tones. He accepted this resignedly, rolling a Black Beauty with skilful rapidity.

I explained that it was my plan to go a little nearer to London, probably stopping in Surrey and then going on into Kent – both of which counties, I knew, were furnished with a fair percentage of Travellers in their population; and many were still said to be itinerant with waggons and horses. It seemed a logical destination.

Feeling exhausted after the tension of the journey, despite the clearness of the roads in comparison with later years, combined with the fact of few encounters with hills of any forbidding gradient, I was anxious to settle the waggon for the night, and tether Megan (as she was named by Ernie Wicker) not too close to any of the other horses.

I accomplished the latter tasks with the minimum of effort and had soon gathered enough wood from the bordering scrub to get a cheering pyramid-shaped *yog* ablaze, my kettle hanging from the crane in the flames. I had transported a full ex-milk churn of water with me. Old-fashioned Traveller-style, I had stored all my crockery, utensils etc., and food, in an old laundry hamper which I had been lucky enough to find.

The day was of that uplifting, spirit rising, variety indicative of the imminence of summer warmth ahead – just visible. The daffodils, which dotted the border of the common, were further proof of the optimism of nature. They are my favourite flower. My neighbours, with great thoughtfulness and consideration, left me to fry some bacon, and boil an onion and some potatoes and cabbage, whilst brewing some black tea. This last diet I found to be sustaining and possibly nutritious: in any event it was a diet to which I obstinately stuck.

After I had completed this repast I lay back on one elbow on the ground for a while, contemplating – through the fire's embers – my position.

It is hard to believe in today's inflationary times, that back in those days it was possible for one person to live quite luxuriously on as little as three pounds a week! And many 'old' Travelling women would boast that they were able to *mong* (beg) virtually *all* their food and clothes at the door when out 'calling' with pegs, lace, or artificial flowers. Their mode of approach did not, of course, bring out the best of any latent generosity of spirit in some of the householders and sometimes little or nothing was their return.

Luckily, however, as I later discovered for myself, if one does not allow one's spirit to be crushed by seemingly constant rejection, eventually one will strike gold, at which all will brighten – one's being is elevated, and weariness drops away: to find oneself the recipient of some sort of return, be it food or cash, has to be experienced to be appreciated. It is, perhaps, the lowest end of the exchange market!

Rousing myself from this reverie I wandered over to the waggon of Old Siddy's brother, Rainbow, which was next to his son-in-law's. The son-in-law nodded and Rainbow gestured toward an upturned galvanised bucket, it being one of several being utilised as fireside seats. I sat down heavily, absorbing the warmth from the fire gratefully.

"I bet you feels better after a bit of 'scran,'" remarked Rainbow, using the old lodging-house term for food rather than the Romani, *hobben.*

"I do," I agreed, adding: "We must've done twenty miles today – long enough I do believe."

"*He* likes to do about two miles at most, if he can," observed the son-in-law eyeing the older man sarcastically.

Several small children came up to the fire intermittently, their sharp eyes and ears endeavouring to pick up any interesting details about the stranger who had arrived in their midst. As is almost universal with the younger children of Travellers, they did not address me, nor did they interrupt the conversation of the adults. Respect was a quality greatly instilled into them from their earliest years. It certainly is a quality that makes both social and family life more equable. Alas, it appears to have largely disappeared amongst many of the *gaujo* families – their interrupting and attention-demanding offspring rendering the time spent with their families by friends to be more a trial of endurance than a pleasure. Very sad, for the children who behave in such an unchecked manner are their own worst enemies. Apart from their parents, who likes them?

"You been here long?" I asked, conversationally.

"We must a-bin *atched akai* (stopped here) fer over a week – an' nobody ain't bin to try an' shift us," Rainbow informed me.

At that moment his wife descended from the waggon, a red-faced woman with black hair and a strongly-built body. She was not exactly handsome but her strength of character showed at once. She was not a woman that I would have welcomed as a mother-in-law.

In later years, after the sudden demise of Rainbow in a motor crash, a passenger in a lorry, she gradually thickened still further in body and soured in nature until she was eventually nicknamed 'Planet of the Apes' after the film which depicted a world that was run exclusively by humanised Chimpanzees and was entitled 'Planet of the Apes.' For some reason that was the name given to her by Travellers, as opposed to that of one of the actual *characters* from the film.

Perhaps it was not *so* peculiar, for, during the nineteen forties and fifties a comedy duo formed in America and became an enormous box-office success in the cinema on both sides of the Atlantic. Named *Bud* Abbot and *Lou* Costello they were a fast-talking ex-music-hall double act who were picked-up by Hollywood with astonishingly profitable results. Bud Abbot, tall, thin, and laconic was essentially the 'straight' man, in conflict with the small, short, tubby little Italian-New Yorker, Lou Costello.

There was, at that time, a rather well known waggon-traveller in the midlands who specialised in tree-lopping. It was, however, an occupation to which he was completely unfitted owing to his being over weight and constantly out of breath. Handicapped by these disadvantages he was loath to venture far up ladders or contemplate contracts that demanded any climbing.

By a freak of nature he was, in every detail of appearance, the double of the little film star. But by an even greater eccentricity, old-fashioned Travellers, who rarely, if ever, visited the cinema *themselves* were nonetheless aware of the existence of the famed couple, but did not know one from the other by appearance. Thus, on hearing the names of Bud Abbot and Lou Costello they clung to the easier name to grasp – Bud Abbott! So, for the following ten years or more, the unfortunate man was saddled with a name, which had no possible connection with him either physically or mentally! 'Bud Abbot' he remained until his death.

It was an example of how, to the illiterate, the apparently simplistic can become somewhat unfathomable.

'Planet of the Apes' approached the fire, nodding at me, and looked at the two men, before demanding, in a thick and almost guttural Hampshire accent:

"Goo an' fetch me some water – there ain't enough for the tea-kittle, an' I wants to wash-up some bits o' things –so goo an' get some now: two of the laziest men I ever seen in all me life," she concluded, glancing at me for sympathy.

I rolled my eyes non-committally, but gave no reply.

Rainbow arose from his bucket seat and placed two rather battered milk churns on to the framework of a pram, kept mainly for that purpose.

"You comin,' Manny?" he suggested to his son in law, who rather grudgingly assented.

Taking Churns to fetch Water

I walked back to my waggon and decided to retire for an early night, as there was much on my mind. I have always been a rather superstitious person, a trait which has not left me. The fact that I had had a successful first journey, landing up with friendly company by chance, without even any minor disasters occurring, was a sure sign of good luck in regard to both waggon and horse. This idea may be scoffed at and ridiculed by those of more sophisticated natures but, through a straightforward following of a set of more or less private principles, I have had no real reason to question my instincts. Indeed, I once bought a brand new truck, and during the first week of my ownership I was pulled-up twice, for no good reason at all, by the police, the clutch burned-out, and an elderly lady reversed into one side – with the strange excuse: "Oh dear, oh dear! You weren't there a minute ago!"

All those events in one week were enough to convince me of the irredeemably unlucky character of the vehicle so I sold it as fast as I could, shouldering the resultant financial loss stoically.

Another of my own possible eccentricities is that once I decide to make for any particular area, either just when travelling about or whether on business, I do not, under any circumstances, change my mind as to where I am headed. To me, as I know, to do so invites ill fortune. Thus, having decided to make for the unknown country of Surrey, then that was where I must go.

It was tempting to stop on with Rainbow and 'Planet of the Apes' for a few days but I was impatient for the Promised Land and the excitement it offered.

I decided to leave the next morning and aimed to spend the night on Blackbush Common, which was then, Rainbow told me, a regular stopping-place for Travellers: from where I would strike into Surrey. Luckily the mare had been shod just before I purchased her so that I was free from worry on that score. As late as the end of the nineteen fifties there were still many small towns and villages in which both smiths and even wheelwrights were yet working – mostly known to the Travellers.

I lit my little Queenie stove and fried a meal of bacon and bread, and one egg crisped as a biscuit. A mug of black tea and I was ready for bed.

It was almost full moon, slightly misty, and the horses munched at the grass and foliage, their plug-chains clinking in the sharp night air. On the road beside the common a very occasional motor vehicle passed on its way home. The comparative peace would be disturbed, however, at regular intervals by the loose dogs of the Travellers forming a pack and racing into the undergrowth behind the waggons, barking in chorus, seeking out real or imagined intruders.

Gypsy Dogs

After the first two or three of those canine forays I managed to ignore them and drifted off to sleep. I woke at about six in the morning to the sounds of birdsong in the bushes, and the stolid munching sound of the horses nearby. I could just make out the tidy silhouette of my little mare across the common.

Rainbow was already breaking up sticks, placing them pyramid-style in the fire place before lighting the morning fire in the dawn light. They were part of good memories of my earliest days in the waggon, times of great happiness and fulfilment.

As I descended from the waggon Rainbow gestured me to join him at his fire where he sat alone – the rest of his family still abed.

"Is you goin' away to *divvus* (day)?" he enquired.

"Yes, I am," I replied.

"Then sit down be the fire, an' have a bit of bread an' meat along've we, young man – there's no sense in you makin' up a *yog* (fire) just for yerself, if you'm goin' away."

"Thank you," I said, "but I can't take your food, with you having a big family to feed."

"Go away!" he exclaimed. "We ain't lettin' you *jal* (go) wi'out some good grub inside you. We've liked yer company; you'm a civil young man an' I shall wish you the best of luck. You got a nice little turnout – so don't chop it away without you're *sure* you've got the best of the deal, 'cos there's a lot of bad men about who'd *chor* (steal) it offen you as soon as look at you."

Within moments 'Planet of the Apes' emerged from the waggon, her broad black features alarming in the first light. However, her humour seemed improved from the evening before and she began frying some bacon on the fire in a large black pan suspended from the crane.

"Gie us a fag, Rainy," she demanded of her husband, who duly obliged.

In exchange she handed him thick slice of bacon enveloped in white bread, and immediately handed one to me also. It may not have been high on the dietary recommendations of many nutritionists but it fulfilled its purpose, namely in assuaging hunger. Two mugs of black tea later and I was ready to harness-up the mare, a little wary of what might lie ahead.

Chapter Twelve

Towards the Future

The little mare pulled willingly and steadily, seeming impervious to the change in circumstance that her new ownership had occasioned. The waggon was undoubtedly light enough for her to manage without difficulty or undue strain even on quite steep gradients, which was of great relief to me. The tap tapping of the horseshoes and the scraping sound of the iron wheel-bonds on tarmac became a normal and familiar sound to my ears.

As we eventually drew abreast of what I realised must be 'Blackbush Common' I noticed a pair of almost matching barrel topped waggons close to one another, about a hundred yards across the ground. A flat trolley was beside them, whilst four good-looking black and white cobs were grazing the patchy grass and vegetation within the lengths of their plug-chains. As always, on catching sight of us, they all stood stock still, their attention fixed unerringly upon us.

Two greyhounds, two deerhound lurchers and an Alsatian bitch with five or six puppies, all emerged from beneath the waggons and, after advancing a few yards, stood barking in unison and in no friendly fashion.

However, upon hearing the dogs a rough-looking man appeared from one of the waggons, whilst seven or eight small children peered from the other waggon.

I raised my hand and he raised his, beckoning me towards him. Feeling a trifle lonely after my solitary journey, and somewhat in need of company, I complied and, leaving the hard road, set off across a rough track towards the waggons. By that time a youth of maybe fourteen had advanced upon the belligerent dogs with a stick and driven them back under the waggons.

As I approached the man came towards me. He was thickset, with longish brown hair, streaked here and there by the elements. His face was broad, almost oriental, and his eyes were faintly slanted. Dressed in a Travellery manner of the time, he wore an aged yoke-backed tweed jacket, cord trousers, turned-up to avoid the mud, and revealing battered old brown jodhpur boots. Around his neck was wound a blue and white spotted silk scarf. At that point one of the dogs raced out as if to attack me.

"Goo-an-lay down, Blue!" shouted the man. Adding to the youth: "Fer fuck's sake tie that *juke* (dog) on, 'fore he kills the man, Tarzan."

On hearing the name Tarzan my memory was jogged. Several times I had heard both Ike and Bronco speak the name. Tarzan was the son of one of Bronco's brothers nicknamed London Mushy – a man to be feared and respected by all accounts.

"Fights like a kickin' horse," Bronco had declared. "If he gets in a public an' gets the beer into him he'll challenge any man there to fight him for five hundred pounds, strike me dead! Yet iffen you meets him most days he's the quietest man you ever seen. He likes to stop most of his time round London – that's why they gid him the name."

I smiled at him and took the chance.

"You'll be London Mushy, I'm sure," I began. "I've heard of you from Bronco – all good things, of course."

He smiled at this, observing, with a pleasant lack of false modesty, "Everyone's heered of me!"

He gazed curiously at me and suggested: "Why not unhitch the mare an' pull-on along of we for a day or two – iffen you ain't in no hurry to gets somewheres."

Always in favour of the unexpected I agreed to his proposal, drawing the waggon on to a level patch a little to the left of his waggons. The ground, barren and over used looking, bore the ring scars of many previous *yogs* (fires) and an unappealing miscellany of human detritus and discarded oddments lay everywhere, miserably at odds with nature, to offend the eye.

Once I had un-harnessed the mare, given her some water and tethered her in a space large enough for her to enjoy the benefit of the full length of the plug-chain, I wandered over to my neighbours' *yog*, where an unexpectedly large number of faces met my eye. Mushy sat surrounded by his children, of whom there were ten, I learnt, Tarzan being the eldest at fourteen. Their mother was out 'calling' with the eldest daughter, and they hoped for her return in the early afternoon. Equally hopeful were they that she would be laden with food, which she would cook for them immediately, despite any weariness she might have felt after a morning trudging from door to door with lace, flowers, or even clothes pegs. A life of ease it was not.

All the children were blessed with the Romani features and colouration of Ike and Bonny. How many of them, I wondered, would choose to remain in a life-style so hard and unyielding – yet so infinitely rewarding – and how many would move into the ever increasing numbers adopting motorisation? Time would tell.

Deeply shocked by my lone journey, without wife or relatives, it took them some time to come to terms with such eccentricity.

"I tell you what, young man," said Mushy. "You needs a good watch dog, getting' about on your own like that – it ain't safe. Now,

"I've got six puppies to sell out of that Alsatian bitch – all pedigree, tho' I ain't got no papers. Now, I've took to you so you can have any one of 'em 'ceptin' the all black un – an' ten shillings is all I'm goin' to ask you."

Looking around at the puppies gambolling about their mother, I picked one, a sturdy dog-puppy, of an even light fawn in colour, knowing he would probably darken slightly with maturity. I agreed to the offer and paid Mushy there and then, arranging to pick up the puppy on my departure.

The puppies were already stand offish toward a stranger, hinting at their latent watchdog qualities.

We talked of Bronco and his family, and they were very interested, especially Tarzan, to hear of Ike's 'new' Bedford lorry and of his progress so early in life.

"That boy'll be a millionaire by the time he's twenty year old," asserted Mushy with conviction.

At that moment a knocked about lorry, laden to breaking-point with scrap machinery, pulled-up on the main road, the driver helping a woman from the cab and leaving her standing with boxes and bags, being assisted by a girl with long plaits and dark complexion. It was Mushy's wife Rosaleen and the eldest daughter, Rosie.

"That's me cousin Albert's boy. He must've given 'em a lift," said Mushy complacently.

"He's after me sister," observed Tarzan.

"Fuck off!" cried Mushy crossly. "She'm only thirteen – too young fer any of that!"

Tarzan looked somewhat offended but thought better of crossing his father.

As the woman and girl drew close I could see how the lorry-owning son of 'cousin Albert' could have been romantically affected by the girl Rosie. She was indeed remarkably beautiful, just about to break into full bloom. Mushy's wife, Rosaleen, was a member of the Lee family from South Wales, and had travelled for all of her life. Child bearing, insecurity, and hard work had all left their mark and her face, though still handsome, was just beginning its downhill run – the tracks and lanes becoming more and more evident with the passing of time.

The mother and daughter gazed at me, in some surprise and curiosity.

"This young man's on his way to Blackbush," said Mushy. "He knows our Bronco and the boys. Knows Old Monty, too."

This appeared to satisfy the woman, who smiled at me in a friendly way before busying herself with the preparation of a family meal. Before commencing that task, however, she handed out sweets to the children who were waiting expectantly. Slightly to my surprise Tarzan seemed anxious not to be ignored.

"Come on, Mam, I was your first baby – don't leave me out," he begged, and was duly rewarded by a slab of chocolate, upon which he munched hungrily.

Mushy had built up the *yog* and soon the black kettle was boiling and tea was brewing.

I made to get up and leave before they started to eat.

"Sit down," ordered Mushy. "You don't think as I'd turn you away from my fire like a *gaujo* do you? Bide there an' have some bread an' meat wi' us. Don't 'fuse or I'll be mortal offended. We've got plenty of victuals to spare, young man."

As was to be my luck in the future I was experiencing the generosity so often meted out by an oppressed and derided people. Soon we were all enjoying a flavoursome stew of vegetables and hunks of bacon. Everyone ate up all that was served to them, with no complaints and evident satisfaction. Upon completion both Mushy and Rosaleen rolled themselves cigarettes of Black Beauty and its faintly sickly scent pervaded the atmosphere – far distant from the times when such inhalation was viewed with horror. (It was, indeed, only a matter of weeks before I myself developed the habit, which I was to maintain for a dozen or more years.) As always, my interest in, and natural ability to memorise, exact relationships amongst Travellers, was one of my greatest advantages in assisting friendships.

I had, in fact, begun to surprise myself at the extent of my knowledge of 'cross pollenisation'! Useless and irrelevant as such knowledge would have been in many branches of society, within the Travellers' world it was invaluable, and remains so. They were greatly interested that I had been stopping with Rainbow and 'Planet of the Apes' – though at mention of the latter they all raised their eyes heavenwards, significantly.

"Funny woman," observed Rosaleen dryly.

With no great fear of malice I nonetheless felt it wise to change subjects. I explained that I had only just started travelling and that I was on my way to Surrey.

"Have you got 'lations up there?" enquired Mushy, hopefully for my sake. For him, too, Surrey was a 'strange country' – it being outside the radius of his normal travels, although, oddly enough, Middlesex and East London were familiar to the family.

Travellers, as a general rule, are more parochial and circumscribed in their movements than is widely realised. There are, of course, a lesser number who wander at will from one end of the country to the other – but they are decidedly exceptions to the rule. When I explained that such was not the case they nodded in awe at my daring to undertake such an excursion into the unknown.

"There's some *beng* (devil) tailed old *chavies* (children) round London," they warned. "But if it's in your mind to go then go you must," said Mushy, and his wife and the entire family stared silently at me.

"Perhaps he'll find hisself a nice young *rackli* (girl)," Rosaleen suggested comfortingly.

I nodded optimistically, and withdrew to my waggon, my thoughts activated to tension-level.

From the time that I had decided to take to the Traveller life-style I had become more and more convinced that I had found what I had sought. I *liked,* admired, and very often *respected,* the people with whom I now seemed to be having daily contact. In those days I was something virtually unique in launching myself in such a manner – hippies, New Age Travellers (so-called), had not been invented. Hence my fascination for Travellers was extreme. It was impossible for me to take even a short journey without being hailed by a differing variety of Travellers – from those in battered lorries out seeking scrap-iron, to those on foot, or others in brand new cars or vans with, ostensibly little of the 'gypsy look' about them. The latter were usually lino or carpet-hawkers and were less in numbers than their manual-labouring brethren. However, despite their respectably smart appearance, I frequently found that conversation with them yielded astounding information of their not too distant pasts, living and travelling in horse-drawn waggons. They were my first contacts with Success, and my admiration knew no bounds: a state of mind, which I have retained throughout my life!

I decided that the next day I would push on and aim for Chobham Common in Surrey where, although not familiar with it himself, Mushy assured me that one could *atch* (stop) for an indefinite period and that there were always 'London Travellers' there, both those still with horses and some mechanised. It sounded promising. I was assured a journey more or less devoid of hills, which was a comfort to me. Smooth tar macadam roads, rubbed even smoother by constant use, are slippery and dangerous to navigate when pulling a heavy load, by equine means, up a steep gradient.

For some unknown reason the little mare seemed to flourish in her new life, her 'rainbow' neck appearing more pronounced and her coat more glossy by the day.

At that time there were still many Travellers of middle age, or elderly, who had but recently forsaken horses, often at the behest of their sons, in favour of lorries or vans. But frequently their hearts were not in the changeover and they still pined for their horses. Indeed they invariably left the motor driving to their offspring – acting as merely knowledgeable passengers when out on business. Thus, whenever they sighted me with a 'pretty little turnout,' they would immediately demand that their drivers halted in order that they could stop for a curiosity-rooted conversation.

I remember on one occasion when a very clean 'cut-down job' – converted from a once respectable Armstrong-Siddeley saloon – shot off the road on sight of me, to the consternation of other road users who had not appreciated the driver's total disregard for signals. As it drew up beside me I saw that it contained two of the blackest Romani men that I had ever seen – a father, the passenger, and his son, the driver, aged about sixty and thirty respectively. They were very 'old fashioned' in aspect and behaviour. Both were dressed Traveller-style in black, narrow-legged suits of heavy tweed, coloured silk neckerchiefs, sturdy brown boots, and black hats. They were polite and expectant, and I asked them to sit down by the *yog* and take a cup of tea. This they did and happily sipped at the drink that I handed them.

"That's a lovely cup of tea, young man," said the father figure. "You can't beat tea what's made over a *yog* – ain't that right, Sam?"

His son readily agreed, gazing fondly at his father in a way that I envied.

It was explained to me that they had a 'bit of an old place' near Andover, and were out on a mission to collect used sacks and bags from farms and factories; later to 'weigh them in' as scrap bagging.

"A poverty living, young man," asserted the father. "You'm lucky to y'earn a crust of bread," he added with a smile. It was the kind of smile I began to realise that was usually on the face of those whose battle with life had generally seen them emerge victorious after a journey of struggle and discouragement: they rightly valued what they had achieved.

They were Old Sam and Sam-boy Lamb. Later I discovered them to be well known and respected amongst Travellers, and *gaujes* alike. As ever, in such company, and that of Aunt Kizzy, I felt a wave of sadness engulf me as they pined for, to them, a long-lost way of life – to which sentimentality only could attach them, their memories forever roseate.

Sam-boy possessed a fine hooked nose, though it unfortunately veered sideways – the result, he explained, of being kicked in the face by a Shetland pony when he was a boy.

"Nearly lost the sight of his dear eye," recollected Old Sam, rolling himself a Black Beauty cigarette of a slender proportion.

"He ain't supposed to have no fags," said Sam-boy. "Doctor says they'll kill him, but he takes no notice."

"I bin smokin' since I wuz a dear little *chavi* (child)," grumbled Old Sam. "Look at me old grannie – still smokin' at ninety-eight! When the dear Blessed Lord wants you He'll call you in."

"There," said his son, sadly.

We gossiped on, the names of many persons of whom I had heard but not then met were mentioned as well as mutual friends or acquaintances. Nothing of the outside world impinged on our conversation. Insularity brought its own rewards.

Eventually they rose to leave and we shook hands. As he did so, Sam voiced a strange farewell that I have since heard all over the country from both English and Irish Travellers: "Hills and valleys never meet – but old friends always do!" A pleasing sentiment, I have always felt.

So saying they climbed into the cab of the once luxurious limousine, its engine purring healthily into life, and slid out onto the road and into the distance. It was not for three years that I met them again, at a 'Horse and Vehicle Sale' near to Salisbury. *Second* meetings, to me, are always something of a trial and risk. But in that instance any foreboding of disappointment was entirely unjustified. As the sales grew to a close we walked across the road to a small and unpretentious public house, 'The Waggon and Horses,' which was already full to overflowing with patrons of the auctions. Consisting mainly of Travellers and old-fashioned 'dealing men' it offered a pleasing spectacle, whilst outside in the spring sunshine were crowded numerous colourfully clad Romani women and children. Their ages varied from the young and beautiful to the ancient and wizened – the latter, however, assuming a beauty of their own, like weathered carvings from a bygone age. We pushed our way into the little bar, greetings from all sides being directed at Old Sam and his son, with affectionate banter from some of the older men.

"Tis too hot in yere for me – I'm gwine outside," declared Sam to his son, adding: "Fetch me drink directly, an' get one for this young man as well – an' don't bide there *rokkering* (talking)!" At this we pushed our way outside again and settled ourselves on a low wall to await our drinks.

A vastly overweight young man in his late twenties heaved himself on to the wall beside us. His face, under a shapeless brown trilby, was red and streaked with sweat. He wore an open dealers' 'smock' coat, old serge trousers tied up with string, and shoes sliced open in order to accommodate bunions of disturbing prominence. His collarless shirt had an evident aversion to the launderer's hand. Nonetheless, from this unprepossessing person there emanated a humorous jollity of spirit, which could not be denied. His hands were large and chubby and from the one embracing a pint pot of black beer there gleamed a huge 'plaited' gold ring of the sort favoured by London horse-dealers.

"Hello, Uncle Sam," he said, smiling broadly. "How be you?"

"Not too bad – for an old un," replied Old Sam. "How's everything at home, Joe?"

"Handsome! thank you Uncle Sam," rejoined Joe politely.

"How's Pemberline? How many *chavies* (children) you got now?" said Sam.

"Lovely, ta. We got three boys, an' another on the way."

"You'll have a football team, Joe, 'fore you'm finished."

"*Kekker* (no)! Uncle Sam. After this one I'm shuttin' up shop," announced Joe, grinning amiably.

"Bought anything here today, Joe?" enquired Old Sam.

"I bought a pretty little coloured colt," answered Joe. "And three old screws, for the glue factory I shouldn't wonder. There's a price, too!"

"We ain't bought nothing,'" grumbled Old Sam. "I reckons my boy ain't goona buy another *grai* (horse). All as is on his mind these days is motors – times is changing, old ways is finished. There's no doubt of that."

In view of my own situation I was saddened to hear such views expressed, though I found, even in my then limited experience, I could see the truth in what was said wherever I looked amongst the Travelling People. Alas, I had just caught the 'fag-end' of a whole way of life – which indeed was virtually to disappear by the end of the nineteen fifties, to be retained by but a handful of its devotees, and later to be adopted, if only temporarily, by a band of human oddments, from a variety of social backgrounds, to be known to themselves as 'New Age Travellers.'

A few of them appeared with genuine Romani waggons and good horses, but the majority seemed to have no idea of the finer points of the life-style which they were trying to appropriate. Ironically, they appeared to receive far more lenient treatment from the local authorities than the genuine Romani Travellers – often being allowed to stop for months on pieces of land from which Romanies had been lucky to catch more than a day. The age of discrimination was not dead.

I said farewell to Old Sam and his son, a little sadly, but very pleased to have seen them again.

The journey to Chobham Common was not too long, and I had no difficulty in recognizing it. It was as described to me by Mushy, and I could see several waggons dotted amongst clumps of gorse bushes, and several coloured horses tethered here and there, whilst, on a clear patch of gravel parking, were at least ten trailers and a number of lorries and vans and the obligatory 'cut down jobs.' For one in my position it was a good sight.

For a Travellers' stopping-place there seemed little activity, but as I pulled on near to the waggons several mongrel dogs and a couple of lurchers came towards me barking uncertainly. At this commotion an ancient man appeared from beside a smoking fire and gazed hard at me.

"Morning," I said.

"Morning," he replied. "Is you pulling-on, young man?"

I explained my situation as best I could, whilst the old man continued to regard me quizzically. His resemblance to Old Siddy was striking, and I discovered that he was yet another brother – their breed apparently to be found in at least four counties.

Once my credentials were unveiled his manner changed and he expressed the hope that I would stop "along of we."

It transpired that almost everyone on the place had gone to a funeral for the day – a grand social event for Travellers.

"I couldn't go meself," explained the old man, "me ticker's fucked-up an' I cain't walk more'n two yards – I'm underneath two doctors an' on 'bout twenty tablets a day – but they cain't do much fer me."

I expressed my sympathy, which he received graciously, adding sadly: "Since my dear wife died I don't care much fer livin'. I'm ready to go whenever the dear Blessed Lord calls me."

Feeling rather depressed I drew my waggon on to a clear piece of ground, un-hitched the mare and tethered her. My puppy, which I had shut in a box in the waggon during the journey, was anxious to be let out so I put the box beneath the waggon and tied him on to a six feet length of chain. He appeared to accept this as part of his new life and, with the characteristic curiosity of his breed, surveyed his surroundings with interest. Despite only being a puppy his guarding instincts were easily discernible. I called him Zeek.

I had soon managed to collect a bundle of 'fuzz-tops' from the surrounding gorse and made up a fiercely burning little *yog*, on which I fried some sausages and bacon which I devoured hungrily – throwing a few morsels in the direction of Zeek. I had placed the kettle on the crane and was about to make some tea when I heard the sound of horses' hooves on the hard road. Sure enough, within moments, a black and white cob appeared, pulling a flat trolley upon which rode five young men. They were all in black suits and neckerchiefs and had obviously come from the funeral. Once having left the main road they set off at a breakneck speed across the common towards us, the wheels of the trolley frequently leaving the ground as it bumped over the deep ruts. With shouts and yips they pulled to a halt beside my fire – obviously astonished at my presence.

Trotting Home

Happily, however, there was no hostility in their eyes and they smiled cautiously. They were, to a man, very 'gypsified' in both dress and features, their angular faces almost olive in colouration: all except one of them were black-haired, their locks slicked back with a watered-down look.

"All right, *mush*?" said the driver.

"Struggling," I replied, grinning slightly.

"Oh mate – ain't we all?" observed the one blonde boy amongst them, in a rather cockney-sounding accent.

I soon learned that whilst the dark boys were all from the waggons, he was from the trailers and was Surrey born and bred: it was an accent with which I was to become more and more familiar in years to come.

"We'll un-hitch the *grai* (horse)," said the driver, "an' we'll walk over an' have a talk later."

Only the blonde boy remained. He was named Wisdom and he and his family travelled almost exclusively in Surrey and Hertfordshire. They had but recently taken the plunge in abandoning horses and waggons for lorries and trailers: the whole family doing so simultaneously. Thus, with his parents, his four brothers and their families, and two sons-in-law they made up a group of at least seven trailers. Safe in the numbers of their own family group they tended to stop together, I gathered.

Wisdom was the 'baby' at only fifteen – though he gave the impression of being nineteen or even twenty, and was still 'at home' with his parents. Blonde of hair and strangely white and haggard, with the palest of cold blue eyes, his face belied his nature, for he was, I soon discovered, humorous and amusing company.

He accepted a roll-up Black Beauty cigarette, lighting it with a brand from the fire, and we smoked contentedly. He told me of the funeral and its size.

"He was a well-liked man, mate," he explained. "Only forty-five an' left a wife an' six *chavies*. Up a tree with his saw an' he only cuts through a power cable! Dropped like a stone by all accounts – dead 'fore he hit the ground."

I expressed my shock.

"The man was a first cousin to me muvver. I never knowed him all that well – but the man never done me no harm. You never seen so many wreathes in all your life – an' too many people to git in the church. They was playin' 'I Done it My Way' an' 'The Old Rugged Cross' on loudspeakers fer us outside to hear."

Obliquely questioning me about myself he seemed quite happy at my replies. I was wearing a thick silver ring and before he left we had a *chop* (swap) – my ring for his silver buckle ring, which I fancied. He had, at first, demanded two pounds plus my ring for his. However, it was but an instinctive try-on, and we eventually met on a straight exchange. There was in the deal a faint feeling of bonding.

Now that I had reached Surrey, an inexplicable aim now achieved, I had to investigate my finances, and consider how I should earn a living. Since taking to the road I had entirely abandoned my previous *choring* (stealing) habits, partly through my altered appearance since adopting Traveller fashions, and partly because in the event of my being arrested all my possessions might well have been lost unless I happened to be staying alongside Romanies whom I knew well.

Thus my field was narrowed. Luckily, and to my surprise, however, Wisdom offered to 'go partners' if I wished to accompany him out looking for scrap iron. At that particular time scrap was not enjoying high prices, which was fortunate for those still with horses and thus without the 'overheads' needed to run a lorry. The plan was to bring the scrap home each day, sort it, clean the non-ferrous metal, and weigh it in at the end of each week in a nearby town, using the services of one of Wisdom's brothers for that purpose, a service he was willing to perform for 'a drink.' All that remained was to find the scrap.

Those in that occupation who were mechanised tended to call at factories, farms, and builders' yards where they were more likely to find full loads, which they bought for cash.

Those with horses, however, employed the 'little apples taste sweet' form of business: that is to say that they (and Wisdom and myself) restricted themselves to back streets in surrounding towns – yielding perhaps a bathtub and piping, and old gas stoves, fires, even lawnmowers or sewing machines – almost all small and easily transportable objects.

Wisdom, not as motor-mad as his brothers, had retained his horse and trolley during his family's changeover, to their astonishment. But it did, in fact, allow him his independence and the ability to earn his own living.

His father Alf, whom I came to know, seemed secretly proud of his youngest son's attachment to the past.

"Takes a good man to keep a lorry on the road," he asserted. "Them boys'll learn that soon enough," he said, gazing with some contempt towards his other sons' miscellany of cleaned-up old vehicles, and fondly at Wisdom's coloured cob munching, on his plug-chain, at the sparse vegetation left on the over-grazed land.

Although my knowledge of the scrap business was, to say the least, not at all inclusive, I decided not to divulge that to my new friend and business partner, Wisdom. I trusted that my natural desire to scavenge would hold me in good stead in my new and most chancy of occupations. As always I felt that my reliance in my own God of Luck must be my salvation. Thus far I had not been let down. Someone once posed the question: What alternative is there to Optimism? Nowhere outside of the Romani life-style is the question more applicable. One exists on its bounty, and without its grace every aspect slides rapidly downhill.

Howsomever, as an old friend was prone to remark, I retired to bed early, on a wonderfully zinging summer's evening, promising to set out with Wisdom the following morning by nine o'clock.

It was a bright and clear morning, early summer, the kind to engender good feelings in all but the most pessimistic. Wisdom emerged from his parents' trailer, an ageing but well preserved 'Carlight Colonial' (then viewed as the 'Rolls-Royce' of trailer caravans), at my approach, and we walked over to where his cob, already harnessed-up and 'in' the trolley, was tethered to a tree.

We both climbed up onto the footboard and set off across the common towards the main road.

Collecting Scrap with the Trolley

"I knows the best little place to call," announced Wisdom confidently, and we set off at a fast trot towards a destination then unknown to me.

Within a couple of miles we turned off the main road into the outskirts of a little town: "A little black town," as I had heard it well described by a Traveller who had spent most of his life within its environs.

Gloomy little streets of an early 'Coronation Street' vintage were the main buildings. Many indeed were undergoing 'improvements' to their interiors – from whence we hoped to reap some rewards.

"You take this side, I'll take that," suggested Wisdom amiably. He took a fifty-six pounds weight from the trolley and affixed a piece of rope to it. The other he attached to the horse's bridle so that, thus anchored, we could be sure of him not moving forward of his own accord and leaving us behind.

Knock on every door was a principle to which we strictly adhered. Perhaps oddly, but definitely superstitiously, I have always found that if I could score even a minor deal at the very first house at which I knocked then my luck would tend to hold for the day. (and for sixty years I have found that it has!)

It was, therefore, with no little delight that I perceived Wisdom dragging an old mangle from the house opposite to mine, whilst I was offered two old iron bedsteads, each with brass knobs on them. The householder, a grim reminder of how little cartoonists exaggerate their subjects, bore an unremitting likeness to the spouse of the fictional 'Andy Capp!' However, her personality was friendly and she seemed grateful that I would remove the beds from her property. New to the experience of calling in 'poverty' areas I was gratified to find the inhabitants so agreeable. Only once, encountering a tousle-headed lump of a man who had apparently just gone to bed after working a night shift, was I the recipient of the brusque dismissal: "Fuck off!" However, I did not allow his apparent displeasure to sink in to my psyche, rather did I marvel at how our collection of 'rubbish' was growing from that one street. Already the trolley was heading towards its full capacity: it was very cheering and something, I thought, of as a good omen.

We eventually reached the end of the street and had stopped to enjoy a Black Beauty cigarette apiece when a small truck drew up behind us. It was a Fordson 15 cwt, almost brand new, painted in a bright pea-green and 'lined-out,' Travellers' style, in red, with wheels to match. From it emerged a man whom I recognised at once as Mervyn Teale, a horse-dealer and half-Romani – his mother being a Buckland. Approaching his sixties, his face was one which could rarely be matched in character. Beneath a green felt pork-pie hat were hawk-like features, bifurcated by heavy valleys running down each cheek, and eyes of a blackness rarely encountered. He sported a red paisley neckerchief and an expensive Traveller-style suit in reticent check tweed. Beside him stood a pale-coloured whippet bitch, which was never out of his company.

"Nice bit o' stuff you boys have found," he smiled appreciatively at our load. "Scrap's gone up a bit today, so you'm on the winning side. How's yer father an' the boys, Wis?"

"Lovely, Uncle Mervyn. I'm glad the scrap's gone up – it'd need to. The poxy stuff's hardly been worth pickin' up – me brothers is all on tarmac or trees."

"They's all right if you can find the right man," replied Mervyn gloomily. But you boys is on the best thing. A steady old livin' an' no overheads."

"I don't know about that, Uncle Mervyn," said Wisdom. "These old *kennicks* (house-dwellers) won't give much away – half of 'em wants more'n we can get for it ourselves!"

"Still in the same place?" enquired Mervyn, changing the subject.

"Yep, nowhere else to *atch* (stop)," answered Wisdom.

"That's a nice little turnout you got, kid," said Mervyn to me, adding: "I seen you passin' through last week, on the top road."

Conversation went on, until Mervyn asked:

"Would you sell that waggon?"

"No, I couldn't do that, not without finding another to live in," I replied, not wishing to part with it unless I could better myself.

"Well, I tell you what – I knows for the prettiest little barrel-top you ever seen. A young woman's got it in a h'orchard agin Tring an' she wants to sell. What's more, I knows a man who'd buy yours at the right money 'cos it's just what he's lookin' out for."

I was thrown into a quandary by his proposition. For whilst I had no special wish to sell my waggon I was, nonetheless, seduced by the idea of a barrel-topped one – a much more pleasing shape to my mind. It would need some consideration.

Mervyn gave me his telephone number and I promised to contact him within a day or so. With that we said our farewells and Wisdom and I decided to return home with our load: it was two o'clock – long enough for a day 'on the iron-cart,' as it was known.

Soon enough we were back by the trailers and off-loading our days' collectings in a space hidden from the road by bushes. It was our own little yard.

"I reckons we got thirty hundredweight there, brother," guessed Wisdom who, unknown to me then, was an astute judge of scrap without the necessity of a weighbridge.

That evening, after cooking myself my usual fried fare, I decided to waste no time and to telephone Mervyn Teale about his buyer for my waggon. I knew that I would have to ask a little extra in order to provide Mervyn with the obligatory 'drink' for 'making the deal.' Meanness on my part would reap no dividends for the future. Mervyn himself, of course, was on to a winner and would hope to draw 'drinks' from us all – to which he was perfectly entitled. We decided that the best course of action would be for him to bring over his prospective buyer, a *gaujo* man I learnt, and we would proceed on the outcome.

After a couple more telephone calls from a call-box it was arranged that Mervyn would bring the man over on the Saturday afternoon from his home in the New Forest.

For the rest of the week Wisdom and I continued our excursions into the realms of back-to-back neighbourhoods with more than expected success. Indeed on the Saturday morning when we weighed-in at a not too distant Scrap Metals Merchant, from the back of one of Wisdom's brothers' lorries, we were more than happy with the payment we received.

The scrap-yard was, by many standards, a small firm but it had its advantages. The proprietor was an aged woman of impressive weight herself, obviously of Traveller blood, with her unmarried son and one youthful assistant. Their method of payment was in itself fascinating: seated in a minute office the ferocious matriarch dispensed cash from a capacious black velvet, draw-string-opening, bag! In those carefree days no paperwork was involved. Bought for cash meant just that! Despite such advantages it could not be said that the atmosphere was anything but depressing. Charismatic feelings it did not evoke. After weighing-in we entered a small public house nearby and enjoyed two or three drinks in the company of a few other Travellers in the same line of business, before heading homewards.

We had been home no more than half an hour when Mervyn's little green truck skimmed carefully across the common. Mervyn and his whippet descended from the truck, accompanied by his passenger. Mervyn had not prepared me for the eccentricity or size of the latter. A man in his fifties, he stood at least six feet six inches tall and, although quite bald, with only a ring of white hair, his face was almost hidden by a vast spade-shaped white beard, which even the most exalted of Father Christmases would have envied. He was, to my mind at any rate, an admirable person.

"*Dordi* (Oh dear)!" said Wisdom under his breath. "An old *Bori Rai* (big gentleman)!" In a bohemian way his appearance pointed towards his social elevation.

"Well, here it is, Sir – a pretty little waggon as I told you, Sir," gushed Mervyn enthusiastically.

The *Bori Rai* stood inspecting my little home with evident approval, and I offered him the information that I was the owner; also pointing out that I could not vacate it for at least a week. The latter condition appeared to be of no moment to him. He seemed to be a nice man.

He appeared to be impressed that I had been on the roads with the waggon only days before, and appreciated its good points when pointed out to him. He had the makings of what I was later to describe as an 'Armchair Gypsy,' a faintly misguided though not offensive breed, increasing greatly in numbers in later years, frequently to be found at Travellers' Fairs, especially *Appleby*.

I had gleaned from Mervyn that no actual price had been mentioned, though he had assured the *Bori Rai* that it would be 'reasonable.' I was thus slightly uncertain as to what to ask, in those bygone days when a hundred pounds was something of a fortune. I could not afford to ask too little, yet I did not wish to frighten him away.

I took a chance.

"This little waggon cost me a lot of money, and I'm not really wanting to sell – but if you like to give me a hundred and twenty pounds you can have it," I remarked in as casual a manner as I could foster.

I heard Wisdom draw in his breath in surprise, and awaited the reaction of the *Bori Rai*. It was not quite what I had hoped for: he was a bit more 'fly' than his aspect suggested. His association with Mervyn Teale may have been of some benefit to him, if not to me.

He looked a little shocked and said, "One hundred and twenty pounds is far more than I could afford."

By bringing in the word 'afford' he estranged himself from the world of dealers. A consideration with which I could only juggle.

"Well, what would your price be – make me an offer and I'll try to accommodate you." I could say no more and I sincerely hoped, for Mervyn's sake and my own that the *Bori Rai* was no 'messer' but was a serious buyer.

"Well, I can offer you eighty pounds," he suggested, a little hesitantly.

"Sorry," I replied at once. "I know that one bidder is worth a hundred lookers-on – but there's no way I'll take eighty pounds. I don't care if I sell the waggon or not."

The *Bori Rai* looked a little hurt and retired to a consultation with Mervyn who was, of course, on my side in view of his commission.

"What do you think?" I enquired of Wisdom who was beside me.

"Don't let him go – the old *mush* has got plenty of *loover* (money), you can be sure of that," observed Wisdom. "Try for a hundred *bars* (pounds)."

It was time for a spiel.

"I tell you what I'll do," I began. "You've come a long journey with Mr Teale and I don't want to disappoint you, *so* – this is my very best offer, to try to help you. As I said, the waggon can't go for a week, *but* if you care to shake hands on the deal, and leave me a deposit, you can have the waggon for a hundred and ten pounds. I can't be any fairer than that, can I Mervyn?"

Mervyn rallied, encouraging the *Bori Rai* as best he could. The latter, however, had one more try.

"I'll give you a hundred and five pounds and collect the waggon in a week's time. I'll leave twenty pounds now – how's that?"

"Okay – done," I replied, shaking his hand rather than slapping hands in the Travellers' custom at the completion of a deal

"A nice little waggon you got there, Sir," observed Mervyn, conscious of his duties as middleman.

I pocketed the twenty pounds and was assured by Mervyn that he would supervise the waggon's removal on the following weekend. In the meantime he furnished me with the address where I would find the barrel-top – which I sincerely hoped would live up to his description. He also gave me the telephone number in order that I could be sure of the owner's presence. Indeed it was only minutes after Mervyn's little green truck disappeared that I telephoned.

I had managed to get myself into one of those nerve-racking and tension-filled situations, which seem to have dogged me for a lifetime. The pleasure of a profitable deal could often spawn anxieties and friction, which would eventually prove the original, though profitable, transaction to have been scarcely worth the ensuing traumas. But for those who enjoy the excitement of buying and selling, 'chopping and changing,' it is its own form of addiction.

At that moment Wisdom arrived on his way to fetch water, with two milk churns on the obligatory pram chassis. I myself had bought two 'fair-ground' galvanised carriers (it was before the day of the universally-adopted stainless steel water 'jacks'). There was a tap in the garden of a cottage bordering the common, inhabited by an old couple who were kind enough to let us fill up once a day.

An ancient Traveller who had spent the previous cold winter there apprised me of the strangeness of the water tap's performance.

"The best tap in the country," he asserted. "In the coldest winter the water comes out freezin' hot, strike me dead."

Towards the middle and end of the nineteen fifties the old-fashioned waggon Travellers were abandoning their picturesque traditional homes for motors and, often small and shabby, trailer caravans. Amongst such people waggons of good build and quality were changing hands for as little as thirty and forty pounds. Even classic Bill Wright of Belper Barrel-tops and huge ornate Reading and Ledge Waggons were un-saleable at anything other than contemptible prices. (Yet today such waggons, like vintage motor vehicles, command prices soaring into the thousands. The old adage 'Today's Rubbish is Tomorrow's Antique' comes to mind.)

My telephone call elicited the information that the owner of the waggon, which was still for sale, would be able to meet me at its location on the day that I suggested.

Suffice to say that all went smoothly on the day and that I bought the waggon, a pretty and well-decorated little barrel-top, from its owner. The latter, to my surprise, proved to be a striking and unusual girl whose features and bearing appeared to me to bear some resemblance to both Virginia Wolfe and Lady Ottoline Morell, apart from her hair which was corn-coloured and of impressive length. Her clothes were flowing, of bright colouration, and of a very personal design. Indeed she appeared to be my ideal.

It was, of course, the girl with whom I would share my life: a person, time demonstrated, of almost too many talents – just a few of which were to receive any recognition in the following decades. It was Beshlie.

My life was irrevocably changed by this encounter. Thus within a surprisingly short space of time we were living and travelling together in the little waggon and embarking on a journey with no end, moving deeply into the Romani life. And, like those admirable people, we were forever altering and improving our possessions, firstly our horses and waggons and then our lorries and trailer-caravans along the way. It was the beginning of a lifetime.

Chapter Thirteen

Beginning of a Lifetime

After acquiring the waggon from Beshlie it was only a matter of days before I moved on to the Watford by-pass, it being less of a distance to the farm of Beshlie's grandparents where she was then living temporarily.

I purchased a remarkably inventive fold-up bicycle from an Army and Navy Stores in Watford. Designed primarily for the Commandos during the invasion of France they were apparently not used in the vast numbers expected, thus huge quantities of unused examples found their way on to the home market: for the smallest of cost they were readily available. The purpose to which I intended its use was the traversing the distance from the by-pass to the farm as speedily as possible – even though I had hitherto been no enthusiast for such a means of transport. (I do, though, hazily remember harbouring a rather unhealthy admiration for the well-developed calf-muscles of a young professional lady cyclist in the distant days of Queen's Park. A legendary 'Sprint' champion, she could regularly be espied hurtling at breakneck speed around the edge of the golf-course, white-blonde hair streaming provocatively in the breeze as she rode, doubtless increasing the fervour of the more elderly club members to re-examine their handicaps!)

I have no desire to impress, or indeed depress, the reader with details of a rather feverish courtship nor epithalamiums. It will, I trust, be enough to say that our 'togetherness' became togetherness, and the wildness of the Watford by-pass was our enviable home for a short while.

It was a period of time during which conditions prevailed that are unlikely to occur again in our age of the organisation and repression of all those on the boundaries of Society. It was before the setting up of official 'Sites' by councils. Therefore, although mass evictions were commonplace in general, there still remained little pockets where no action was taken until the quantities of Travellers swelled to unimaginable numbers. The Watford by-pass was, just then, one of those 'pockets.' Along its length there were Travellers in a variety of dwellings. Some had been there so long that they had erected little huts as accommodation, others were in tarpaulin-covered rod-tents, or 'Benders' as they were sometimes called. But the majority were living in either waggons or trailer caravans. Even there, in conditions some might view as verging on squalid, the changeover to mechanisation was evident.

Rod or Bender tent

Many were at the halfway stage with colourful waggons from their horse-drawn lives, and lorries, 'cut-down Jobs,' or old vans drawn in alongside them.

Beside most of such turnouts there also lay a heap of scrap-iron, waiting to be sorted prior to its 'weigh-in.' To the initiated it was a homely sight.

I managed to find a vacant space and guided the waggon and horse off the main road on to a patch of ground that only the most optimistic of persons would describe as unsullied by the blight of previous human presence. However, two things were in our favour. We had brought a full churn of water with us, and the grass verge opposite to us was surprisingly un-grazed. Before many minutes the mare was plugged-on and munching happily after a drink of water.

To one side of us was a tiny, semi-derelict little trailer, no occupants then being present, with the remains of a fire on the ground and a large kettle-iron hanging over its dead ash.

Traveller Children – Mending the Sling

On the other were four trailers of no great charm, though all were gleaming in their polished state. Apart from one woman and five or six straggly little children, and four lurchers, there appeared to be no one else yet back from their days' labours. Beside the furthest trailer a large 30 cwt Bedford van was parked. It was hand-painted in two tones of mushroom, the latter being a favourite of some Travellers endeavouring to give a 'select' complexion to their vehicles. Others, of course, threw such caution to the winds and had their vehicles in the traditional colours of maroon and straw, often 'picked out' in bright red, with designs of buckled-belts surrounding the owners' initials upon the doors. The latter convocation of 'gypsy' motifs did, I confess, attract me personally. However, I could appreciate the logic of those Travellers to whom the 'gypsy look' would sensibly in their eyes, present yet one more obstacle in the minds of those with whom they were dealing. To earn a living was, and is, in any form of freelance enterprise involving the act of knocking on doors, a task of sustained dedication, not for the pessimistic or faint-hearted.

It was not long before we had temporarily established our little home, and thrown down some bedding under the waggon for Zeek, by now almost full grown, and already a good watchdog within his own territory. The summer was still hanging heavily in a dry and dusty heat.

The traffic on the by-pass was quite dense and noisy throughout the entire day and half way through the night. There were no more than four hours in the twenty-four in which its presence was not heard. It was a far cry from *the wind on the heath*, a mirror of how life was becoming degraded, with no apparent signals that it could improve. Nonetheless, there was about the spectacle of so many families, in such varying homes, stretching far along the roadside, a certain theatricality in the face of adversity. Life was being carried on publicly and privately, with little or no attention being given to the constant stream of passers-by, nor even to the spasmodic cries of 'gyppos' from their cars. Any hostility was a two-way matter: the Travellers, as always, regarded the *gaujes* as being of little interest – their only use being to afford a living to the Travellers.

Gradually our neighbours returned with their scrap-laden lorries and parked beside their respective trailers. They turned out to be a family with the strange name of Bones. There was an old man and woman, their lorry driven by their youngest son, Wally, who was still 'at home.' Also present were their two married sons with their two trailers, the fourth trailer belonging to their daughter and son-in-law. It was evident that they had all enjoyed a 'good day' as each lorry was heavily laden – especially one belonging to their 'lucky' son Sam which was almost 'sitting-up' under the weight of its cargo, mostly of cast-iron fragments.

They were undoubtedly 'London Travellers,' spending most of their time moving constantly between the London Boroughs, Surrey, and Sussex. The elderly father and mother, Will and Darkus, were in their sixties though could easily have passed for octogenarians, especially Darkus. Her features, very Romani-looking, were pitted and lined to an almost unimaginable degree: a lifetime's toasting before outdoor wood fires, crouching over the *yog* to cook their meals, combined with a heavy addiction to Black Beauty, had combined to take their toll. Even the most blatant cosmetics' publicist would have been hard put to offer the chance of any benefit being displayed by even diligent use of their products! Her features were the most life-battered that I have ever encountered. Her spirits were probably not improved by her husband's constant assertions that he was about to find himself a new and more attractive partner. No Adonis himself he nonetheless appeared to view his chances in such a quest merely a matter of time. Oddly enough, genes will out and his peculiarly lascivious nature appeared to have been inherited by his sons – all of whose wives lived in a perpetual state of anxiety or fury over their husbands' behaviour.

Besides Wally, still only seventeen and single, there were sons Sam and Ben and their families of six children apiece. Their married sister Evie and her husband Bob, with no less than eight children were also with them. Despite their prodigious breeding programme, however, it emerged that Evie and Bob were 'apart' and contemplating divorce. Thus Bob was living in the old Bedford Van whilst Evie and the children were in the trailer. The two parents were not on speaking terms, and the children had taken their mother's side.

Old Will and Darkus had lost no time in informing me of the situation, and were not slow in expressing their distaste for their soon-to-be ex-son-in-law, who had apparently been caught in a passionate embrace with a woman in the kitchen of whose house he had been removing an old boiler for scrap.

"Fuckin' bastard," mused Will. "*Took* one old boiler an' *had* the other!"

"He should be transported or burned on the fire," seethed Darkus in a refreshingly archaic view of punishment not often voiced, one would imagine, on the Watford by-pass.

I had glanced at Bob and was struck at once by his strangeness and near-maniacal visage – wolf-like and cruel.

Apart from Wally and old Darkus I did not find them attractive as a family though luckily they seemed quite lacking in hostility towards me. Indeed Ben, the eldest, told me privately that he had been the victim of so many fines for motoring offences that he was seriously pondering on whether or not to return to horses. Should he do so, he assured me, he would like to travel with me: to go 'down country' (by which he meant Somerset and Devon) was his aim, to which I agreed.

It was not to be, however, as Ben decided to try his luck in the field of tar macadam laying – an occupation to which increasing numbers of Travellers were turning, with some success – and found it to his liking.

He had a certain unscrupulous charm which he used to great effect. (By the end of the nineteen sixties he was travelling in great style with a new trailer, new TK lorry and a luxurious limousine as well. Of the family his was the story of the most spectacular success, and I was pleased to see it.)

It was, alas, comparatively brief, being cut-short by his increasing addiction to drink, coupled with a harrowing accident in Cornwall. The latter, although causing no serious injury to any of the family, nonetheless saw the complete destruction of his new Westmorland Star trailer, only a few weeks old, and his almost new lorry. The trailer was uninsured, and the lorry insurance was out of date – thus in one horrific accident his whole worldly possessions were completely destroyed. He was never the same again, nor did he manage to rise to his former glory despite valiant efforts.

It fell to his brother Sam, having taken the same path, with the added advantage of his six sons – aged from ten to eighteen – to help him. His income, and indeed workload, was prodigious and such devoted toil brought its own reward.

His fame was in no way decreased when, after buying one brand new limousine in the morning, he decided that it did not meet with his full approval so part-exchanged it in the afternoon for a more expensive model! It is of such stuff that *modern* legends are made!

The Bones family as a whole were contemptuous of those with turnouts inferior to their own, yet unmistakeably jealous of anyone who outdid them in that respect. It seemed unlikely that such an outlook could bring them much satisfaction.

So it was that their contempt and disgust for the dwellers in the battered little trailer to one side of us was unadulterated by the faintest degree of pity or sympathy.

"Fuckin' Scotch cunts," explained Wally to me. "They *monged* (begged) that old tailer off a *kennick* (house-dweller). Fuckin' rubbich! Me bruvver took pity on 'em an' towed it back – he's silly like that; too good-hearted."

"How do they get about, then?" I enquired.

"You never sin nuffink like it!" exclaimed Wally, rolling his eyes. "They got an' old *mule,* on my life, a fuckin' mule! An' a little trolley on blow-up rubbers – that's what they come here with, an' an old bender. Poverty! You never seen nuffink like it – but I s'pose they're all like that in Scotland. Not *proper* Travellers – me dad calls 'em hedge-mumpers. I wish they'd fuck off – they're up drinkin' half the night. The woman's wusser'n him – both fuckin' *dinilos* (fools), mate. Wait till you sees 'em – I bet you'll shift right away!"

I had only met a very few Scottish Travellers. Although the ones I met were quite pleasant they mostly lacked the indecipherable quality enjoyed by Romanies, even those of the Bones fraternity. Their most frequent colouration – freckled red skin, ginger-gold hair and bright blue or pale grey eyes – set them apart from the Romani people.

Later in life I discovered that, as with English Romanies, there were greatly differing standards of life enjoyed by their kin – from extreme 'poverty' to house-owning opulence and business achievements on an impressive scale.

It was rewarding for me to meet one Scottish Traveller family with whom I became close friends for over twenty years. Despite many strangely *gaujo* characteristics, and a degree of erudition, they were without doubt Travellers. I watched their progress with admiration and affection. Unfortunately they effected a distance from English Travellers, whom they chose to dislike in general, isolating themselves in their choice of stopping-places whilst in this land of their chosen exile.

At that moment I heard the muffled sound of hooves and perceived, with no little astonishment, the sight of two shabby and heavily muffled figures on the footboard of a small four-wheeled trolley, drawn by a black mule at no great pace. Their surprise at seeing myself and Beshlie was no less than our own it seemed.

As they came level I discovered them to be a man and woman of middle age, both of them possessing features that had long-since lost the battle against the effects of fire, weather and alcohol. They were the archetypal 'dossers.' They were not the company I would have chosen as neighbours, but I tried to make the best of it.

They were going under the names of Wully and Bessie McPhee – but I had no particular desire to know whether or not the nomenclature was true or false. I was beginning to take the usual Traveller stance of judging people by their possessions!

We gazed at each other.

"'Tis no like summer, maister," observed the woman mournfully, staring reproachfully at a grey cloud which momentarily obscured the sun's rays. It was, in truth, a perfect summer's day – a little too hot if anything.

Upon their trolley lay a tiny heap of worn-out ragged clothing, the apparent result of their day's 'tatting' around the houses.

"How's your luck?" I enquired.

"Nae fuckin' good," grunted the man in a guttural and husky voice. "I ken I've never met more balm-pots an' wee ring-tails than we've been across today. They'd no gie you salt for a tater!"

Their negativity and defeat dripped from them like damp rivulets on a cellar wall. Their mule, too, echoed their manner, standing immobile as though dazed in the sunlight.

After some minutes they un-harnessed the docile animal and tethered him across the road near our mare. Fetching a few sticks that they had evidently stored beneath their trailer they lit a small *yog*, frying themselves a singularly acrid-smelling piece of meat, a strangely purple-tinged flesh, and devoured it hungrily with lumps of white bread. Instead of tea they produced a three-quarter's full bottle of Scotch whisky which they slopped into old enamel mugs, slurping the liquor down with that mixture of guilt and enjoyment which so often afflicts alcoholics. Their already alcohol-fuelled systems soon began to feel the effect of the new 'shots.'

"Will you no come over an' take a wee drink, Hen?" asked the woman in the pushy manner that so often besets the would-be social drinker.

"I will in a while, it's a bit too early for me," replied Beshlie, working towards not antagonising the woman, who, however, grunted irritably at the rebuff.

They had soon begun singing together, strange indiscernible Scottish songs in accents so thick that their meaning was lost on us. After an hour or so, the bottle empty and thrown aside, the couple collapsed into drunken slumbers by the embers of their tiny fire, temporarily freed from the worries of their little world.

The next morning we were awoken by curses and clattering, shouts and screams. Our relief knew no bounds when we discovered that the benighted pair were packing their few belongings onto the trolley, already had the mule harnessed-up, and were about to leave.

I jumped down from the waggon and went to bid them farewell. They made no mention of their previous evening's behaviour, and neither did I. We parted as though we were the best of long-standing friends, despite having spent so short a time in their company. Indeed as they pulled their little turnout off the grass and on to the road, in the face of the morning rush-hour traffic, I felt a small pang of regret at their going. But at least, I recognised, I still had their little begged-trailer to remind me of them, value-less eyesore that it was.

In a matter of a couple of days, however, I began to feel restive and anxious to find more salubrious surroundings. We agreed to move towards the Guildford area, knowing that at that time Travellers could still stop more or less unmolested for a week or two.

Just before we left a small square shaped 'Dorset' waggon pulled-in on the spot vacated by the Scottish people. They were indeed their very opposite in appearance and behaviour. They were 'proper' English

Romanies, with Cambridgeshire accents. The man was small, dark featured and pleasant-looking, in a 'rustic' striped shirt with no collar, a red silk *diklo* (neckerchief) and black tweed waistcoat and trousers: he appeared to be in his fifties. The woman, her black hair in two long braids, was very old-fashioned-Traveller looking. She did not try to look anything but 'gypsy' – it was good to see. She appeared to be ten or more years younger than the man. Also, following exactly in her mother's features, was a small girl of maybe six or seven at most: she too wore her black hair in two braids.

They were a nice, if slightly sad, little family – and although we spent only haft a day in their company we left them, feeling better and happier for the experience.

They had themselves often stopped on the 'Hog's Back,' our destination near Guildford, and although viewing it as a little 'wild' nevertheless assured us that it was a good *atchin tan* (stopping-place).

We set off directly, I myself light hearted at the prospect of new unknown territory: optimistic as ever. Beshlie, as ever, rather more pessimistic than myself, was more cautious in committing herself. Was it possible that the old adage, *opposites attract*, was more than mere legend? Time would tell.

Epilogue

Seated in our trailer now, in the early years of 2000, I am scarcely able to realize the hardships and complexities that have been our lot since first taking to the roads with a horse and waggon in the bygone era of the nineteen fifties. A vanished and perhaps not to be entirely mourned period of time, just prior to the onrush of 'progress' which engulfed a whole way of life for Romanies. Horses and waggons disappeared and in their place came mechanisation in the form of lorries and trailer-caravans. It was not really, however, until the late 'fifties that more than a very few manufacturers grasped the fact that a new market for 'flash' trailers, built to jazzy and rococo specifications to suit the taste of Travellers, was there for the taking.

Indeed most Travellers, before the advent of such specialised manufacturers, had been forced to make do with ordinary, often small, *gaujo* (non-Romani) tourers – frequently damp and not insulated – which were totally unsuitable as permanent dwellings.

The first move toward improvement was the installation of hard-fuel stoves which, if filled to capacity with coal or coke, would keep all but the worst condensation at bay. Indeed, Beshlie and myself, having become motorised in about nineteen fifty-nine, had managed by 1962, after a variety of inferior damp tourers, to acquire a brand-new Sprite Major which was fitted with a small coal-burning stove and also an excellent 'tip-up' bed which by its nature defied damp. Pulled with a knocked-about old Bedford lorry we felt, nonetheless, proud owners.

During that spell our lives were indeed precarious and difficult to maintain, even at that low standard. But, of course, we were propped-up by the double advantages of good health and youth. (As an aged Traveller once remarked to me on the above conditions: "Iffen the dear God made anything better he must've kep' it fer Hisself!)

When we first took to motors and trailers we stopped exclusively on roadsides and old commons, in much the same way as we had done with horses. And with the mass changeover at that time by old-fashioned Travellers all over the country, what remained of the habitual stopping-places, once attractive with colourful waggons, were by then usually stuffed with dull-looking little tourers, old motor vans and 'cut-down jobs.' They were, to many, a faintly dreary sight.

It was something to which there was no alternative: the idea of 'Gypsy Sites' had scarcely been mooted as a possibility to abate the 'problem.' Suddenly being brought into prominence as a 'problem' for local authorities it was interesting and somewhat depressing to observe their reactions.

Oddly, and quite without rationality, many councils took an obnoxiously racist approach, both misguided, and worse still, misinformed. Their curious assertion being that the majority of the Travellers were not *'real'* Romanies but merely 'slum-dwellers who had taken to the life-style!' A quite extraordinarily inaccurate assessment – and one that could easily have been disproved if they had entered any of the rough and ready trailer caravans, the occupants of which, almost without exception, could have produced pictures of their immediate ancestors, or even of themselves, living in traditional 'Gypsy Caravans' – thus fulfilling the councillors' idea of the archetypal Romani. It was more than depressing to note that their fallacious beliefs were frequently mirrored in the tabloid newspapers of the popular press. If nothing else their argument was that of snobbery and racism: I doubted, or hoped, that it would not have been upheld in later decades – a hope that I fear proved to be not entirely justified.

Beshlie and myself, not wholly divorced from bouts of both good and bad fortune, spent our early years struggling under ferociously primitive conditions – cooking over stick fires, living almost entirely out of doors in all weathers, moving constantly at all times, 'chopping and changing' a surprising number of waggons, and horses too, before graduating to motorisation.

In that sphere, as with waggons, we started humbly – never dreaming of the greater glory which would play about our heads from the middle nineteen sixties onwards.

I endeavoured to describe our life with waggons in my book *Smoke In The Lanes* in 1958, which although critically acclaimed, did not bring me more than a flimsy financial return. I also wrote *Whichever Way We Turn* in 1964 in which I attempted to describe our changeover from waggons to trailers. Again, a small critical warmth, but even less reward than my first book.

I realised that by living as and with Travellers, and earning my living by door-to-door Travellery pursuits, I could rely on being far more amply reimbursed than I seemed to be able to achieve as a writer of limited 'popular' appeal.

And so it was that Beshlie and I continued the long slow climb, enjoying competing in the exclusive 'rat-race' peculiar to Romanies. As the increasingly rococo and splendidly vulgar trailers appeared with infinite ornamentation (the Vickers and the Westmorland Star being the two most sought after), we managed to acquire them ourselves.

To some *gaujo* people, of course, such behaviour was in no way admirable, being dismissed out of hand – usually, I found, by those very people who would have been incapable of earning enough money to buy them for themselves. Envy takes on many disguises!

Alas, however, by the 'eighties' inflation, and various other esoteric economic factors, had prevented any more of such coach built trailers from being built – their cost would have been prohibitive. So, two firms, Buccaneer and Roma, each produced a kind of economy version of the first two. These became very desirable and were lighter and easier to tow, as I know from the experience of owning both models. Although quite 'flash' both inside and out, they nonetheless lacked the unadulterated splendour and quality of design of either the Vickers or Westmorland Star.

Strangely enough, two or three German manufacturers then had some considerable success with what were, in effect, large *gaujo* Tourers, with no solid fuel stoves, nor stainless steel appendages. Rather than the latter decoration the Germans appeared to have an affection for plastic, demonstrated in abundance. Even though, up to the present, the German 'Tabbart' and 'Hobby' trailers are to be seen in increasing numbers there is no great feeling of pride in ownership (as we ourselves discovered). Glossy and efficient they may be, but there is no craftsmanship or 'knick knacks' upon which to cast one's eyes when at home, resting, perhaps, after a hard day's toil!

As a kind of reaction, maybe, there has been a great revival of interest by Travellers in the older trailers of the nineteen seventies and eighties. One is delighted to see increasing numbers at all the Travellers' fairs, usually in pristine condition and a tribute to their makers and their present owners. In keeping with such a fashion Beshlie and myself have rid ourselves of our 'plastic' trailer and have bought a 20ft Buccaneer of reasonably ornate exterior and extremely ornate interior – including the imposing house-size 'Parkway' fire stove.

Today, in mid-winter, as I sit before its comforting glow, in a haze of white-grained Formica, cut-glass full-length mirrors, and generously applied additions of stainless steel appendages and ceiling-strips, with bunks of velvet and embossed in floral patterns, and a carpet the like of which would rarely be seen outside of a cinema foyer, I smile to myself and think how lucky am I to appreciate such ornate simplicity!

The Author with his Buccaneer Trailer

After the passing of fifty years since the publication of my first book *Smoke In The Lanes* I became increasingly aware of my own mortality – a lifetime of 'ducking and diving' beginning to take its toll. Time became my enemy. I therefore decided to submit myself once more to the pain of literary endeavour – for me never an easy task to propel works into erudite poignancy. But on consideration I decided to attempt the almost impossible feat of recording the 'climb' made by Beshlie and myself in the lifestyle of modern-day Travellers with motors and trailers.

It was an attempt of a rather hazardous nature, treading an undoubtedly delicate path. It is a way of life in which possessions, in the form of vehicles and trailers, have to be constantly replaced – either out of necessity or, more commonly, to 'keep up' with the fast-flowing changes within the *fashions* of the life. All of which is costly and for which sufficient money has to be earned. Oddly enough the Travellers' ability to survive under conditions in which stability plays little part makes their achievements even more remarkable. That ability to survive, and even prosper, despite frequent persecutions and evictions, would seem to evoke neither curiosity or surprise in the minds of newspaper reporters. The latter indeed constantly publish outrageously biased and ill-informed articles of such prejudice and racism that they would not be allowed were their targets anyone other than Travellers.

They seem unable to comprehend that Romanies, along with everyone else, have moved forward with the times. Whatever their appearance may suggest, their Romani blood has not diminished just because they are no longer living in 'gypsy caravans.' (One could ask: Is the man ploughing his fields with a new tractor a *real farmer*? Shouldn't he be using Oxen?!)

In 2007 my last book before this one was published. I called it *Beneath The Blue Sky* – a line from the old Traveller song 'The Romani Rai.' Although badly edited, I feel that, by and large, it presented one man's truthful view of the travelling life over forty years from personal experience – and as such is unique, to the best of my knowledge.

Refusing approaches from two separate national newspapers who wished to print articles about me I probably diminished its sales, but I was not unduly distressed as I nowadays value privacy more than publicity.

In the contemporary age of 'celebrity' culture such reclusive behaviour might well outrage those whose main ambition appears to be the acquisition of 'fame' at any price, often disregarding their own complete lack of any form of discernible talents whatsoever. As for myself, I have discovered, after decades of unexpected events, I prefer to look backwards – in a kind of perpetual reverie – than hazard any guess as to what the future holds. The battle with Nature can be fought with varying degrees of success – but inevitably one will finally be crushed by the sheer weight of Time. The latter becoming one's most implacable Enemy.

Alas, almost all of the people of whom I have written are long since dead and buried. Just their children remain. My lifelong friend Ike is no more; collapsing from a heart attack at the age of sixty-four. He married a Romani girl and was the father of two sons, both taking his good looks and agile mind. Both successful and enjoying the profits from their 'car-fronts' along the South Coast.

As was foretold Ike achieved a great deal. He eventually founded a Commercial Vehicle-selling business near to Bournemouth which prospered to an undreamed-of degree. This allowed Ike to live in a seaside mansion of Malibu overtones, drive a Rolls Royce, and generally lead an existence in the kind of luxury which his grand-parents would have found impossible to imagine.

His father Bronco, and his mother, had both died a few years before. *All* the older relatives were long since in their graves.

Bonny, who rather surprisingly, married a *gauji* girl from Poole, remained in the scrap-metal business, with his own well-equipped yard, succeeding financially though not in the league of Ike. Unfortunately for him he had no son to take over as he had three daughters, two of whom had set up their own hair-dressing salon within Bournemouth's 'West End.' The third, however, inherited more of her Traveller roots and did indeed marry back into a Romani family, though with a settled-down history. The son-in-law, Caleb, who was greatly liked by Bonny, welcomed his chance to enter the family business, thus allowing Bonny, who was already in failing health, the opportunity to relax his rigid working code a little. He was suffering from a number of bodily malfunctions, including frequent and sever attacks of 'branchitees' – to which all of his older relatives had been prone.

His face, once so handsome and carefree, had become sunken and haggard, his breathing hard and wheezy. On the last occasion that we met I could see death in his face. Within weeks I was at his funeral.

It was as though I had witnessed a whole way of life being destroyed for the older people, and so many of their descendants never managing to adapt fully to a sedentary life. Even those, like Ike and Bonny, who did *ostensibly* succeed, were still living on the periphery of society and not really *feeling* part of it.

Notwithstanding, by and large, Romanies are possibly in a better-placed and stronger position than they have ever been, despite fairly frequent attacks on them from the lower end of the tabloid press, mainly by self-inflated columnists with little knowledge of the subject: sensation-seekers with little or no regard for the truth.

However, one's faith in the abilities of Romanies to adapt themselves to the changing face of society, with the ebullience which has enabled them to survive centuries of persecution, cannot fail to be buoyed up if one attends any of the Travellers' Fairs, such as Appleby, Stow, or the ever-growing Kenilworth Horse Fair. At any of those gatherings one can see the spirit of the gypsy people flourishing, all present fully appreciative of their heritage. I recently read in a book: "A once proud race has been brought to its knees."

This is just not so, and only encourages those who continue (with misguided but good intentions) to present the Travellers as 'Victims,' in a rather patronising manner. 'Survivors' would be more apt.

Only in the life of Jews does there seem to be any parallel. Yet through my lifelong association with Travellers, as a sort of insider/outsider my own spiritual rewards have been immeasurable: it has been their company, unlike the regimentation of life as a 'Conscript,' which really 'Made a Man of Me!'

The Author with Jubilee Trailer and his First New Lorry

Lorry, Waggon and Trailer

The Author Today

Other Books by Dominic Reeve

Smoke in the Lanes 1958 and 2003

No Place Like Home 1961

Whichever Way we Turn 1965

Beneath the Blue Sky 2007

Lightning Source UK Ltd.
Milton Keynes UK
UKOW04f1933100917
308920UK00001B/50/P